WEIRD

CRUDE

FUNNY

&NUDE

The Bible Exposed

TOM FRENCH

Illustrations by Angus Olsen

WEIRD, CRUDE, FUNNY, AND NUDE: THE BIBLE EXPOSED

Copyright © 2018 Tom French
All rights reserved

ISBN 978-0-6483041-0-4
Ebook ISBN 978-0-6483041-1-1

First published 2018 by Frendrussi Press
Sydney, NSW, Australia

Cover design by Emily Sandrussi
Cover and internal illustrations by Angus Olsen
Internal design and typesetting by Sam Williams

For Emily,
I love you like the mountains

Contents

Introduction

Imagine that you're sitting in church. It's a pretty normal service. You've just done some singing, had some announcements, and now it's time for a sermon. Maybe you're a bit bored. Maybe you're looking forward to hearing someone talk about the Bible for the better part of an hour. Maybe you're wondering if your crush noticed when you accidentally liked (then quickly unliked) one of their Instagram posts from two years ago. Whatever you're feeling, you're not prepared for what happens next.

The preacher steps up to the lectern and says, "Today we will be looking at the deep eternal truths one can learn from a fat man who gets stabbed and poops himself."

How would you feel? If you're anything like me you'd sit up, you'd switch your brain on, and you'd be ready to go. Maybe you'd even jump up and shout, "Preach it, Pastor!"

What if the next week the preacher spoke about interdimensional angel sex, followed by a sermon on some women who lusted after men with "genitals like donkeys", capped off by a message about the streaker at Jesus' arrest? Maybe you'd know for sure you were in the right church and God was finally speaking your language.

If that's how you would feel, this book is for you. There are so many good things in the Bible but some of them get neglected. Understandably, we don't spend a lot of time getting taught in church about such things as the exact dimensions for building a piece of holy furniture. We're more often taught about the time Jesus destroyed a bunch of furniture. We spend a lot of time talking in church about how Jesus calmed the wind and the waves, but we don't spend much time studying the only incidence of flatulence in the Bible. This book is more the latter than the former. Less obscure rules and instructions, more obscure body parts and bodily functions.

2 Timothy 3:16-17 says this:

> All Scripture is God-breathed and is useful for teaching, rebuking, correcting and training in righteousness, so that the servant of God may be thoroughly equipped for every good work.

What these verses mean is that every single part of the Bible is from God. He was present when it was written, inspiring the human authors to write exactly the right thing. That means that when the writer of Genesis wrote about the time Uncle Noah got drunk and fell asleep naked, they were writing the word of God. When the writer of 1 Samuel wrote about David's special forces' task to cut off the foreskins of one hundred men, they were writing the word of God. When Paul wrote in Galatians that he wished people who were spreading lies about God's salvation would cut their genitals off, he was writing the word of God. Just because these are rarely spoken about in church doesn't mean they are not God's word.

What's more, because they are God's word, that means that they must be "useful for teaching, rebuking, correcting and training in righteousness, so that the servant of God may be thoroughly equipped for every good work." The purpose of this book is to show you that even the bits of the Bible that appeal to your juvenile mind have great things to teach us about who God is, what he has done and how we can live for him. Also there are jokes.

Who Should Read This Book?

Because I'm greedy, I want everyone to read this book. I want it to sell millions of copies so I can buy a mansion and a private jet. But God will more likely choose to answer the prayer of the writer of Proverbs and give me neither poverty nor riches. There's a good chance if you're reading this it's because you're related to me, or I gave it to you for Christmas because I bought too many copies of my own book. Feel free to stop reading now and just pretend you read the book. I won't know.

However, if you do have an interest in exploring the bits of the Bible with nudity, toilet humour, zombies, and teleporting, this is the book for you.

I have written the book with the assumption that most people reading will have an active faith in Jesus. But if you don't - if you don't even believe that God exists, if you never go to church, if you know nothing about Christianity - that's fine. Hopefully I've written in such a way that anyone can understand what I'm writing about, even if you disagree. You can read it only for the jokes if you'd like - but keep an open mind, because who knows what could happen? You might just meet with God while reading the story about the bears that maul forty-two teenagers for mocking a bald man. Stranger things have happened, like a bear mauling forty-two teenagers for mocking a bald man.

However, if you don't appreciate scatological humour, or funny euphemisms for body parts and bodily functions, this is not the book for you. There are plenty of those in the pages that follow. If you're unsure, I've written an easy test. I'm going to write a few words and if, by the end of the following list, you are feeling uncomfortable, offended, distressed, or appalled, it's safe to assume this is not the book for you. Feel free to go read some Timothy Keller, he's a better writer but with less jokes.

Here we go:

- Bum
- Dong
- Willy
- Fart
- Poo
- Boobs
- Jiggly bits

How did you go? Are you still with me? Are you eager with anticipation for all the comedic and theological gold that is to come? Excellent! Read on, dear reader!

How to Enjoy the Book

I'm not going to tell you what to do. If you have a paper copy of the book, you might have it to prop up a wobbly table, or use it to start a fire on a cold winter's night as you try to woo the person of your dreams (in an entirely biblically appropriate and consensual way). I don't mind, you bought it, I've got your money, do what you want with it.

On the other hand, if you actually want to read the book, then feel free to read it all the way through, or pick and choose the chapters that appeal to you. Each chapter is pretty self-contained so the casual chapter drop-in won't confuse you. However, if you read it all the way through you'll get a better idea of the big picture of the Bible as the chapters are arranged in chronological order.

When you do read a chapter, I would recommend having a Bible on hand and reading the passage I write about, and then keeping it open beside you. I have included parts of the passage within each chapter (NIV 2011 version for you Bible translation nerds), but it's still good to read stuff in an actual Bible. This will help you to see Scripture in its native context, and if you have a different translation, it will help give you a broader understanding of the text.

Generally the funny bits are at the beginning of the chapter and then I show you what we can learn from the passage at the end (though I try to spread jokes throughout). If you're anything like me you might be tempted to skip the parts that aren't funny, but you'll miss the best bits. This book is designed to show how the weird, crude, funny, and nude bits of the Bible can teach us God's truth just as well as any other part of God's Word, but you won't see that if you stop reading halfway through a chapter.

Lastly, I would suggest you read the footnotes. This isn't because they are full of boring references (though there are one or two of those) but because some of my best material is in there and I don't want you to miss out on any of my favourite jokes – I spent a long time thinking about them. The footnotes also include other tidbits of information and tangents of inquiry that don't quite fit with the flow of the chapter. Plus the only time the word nipple is used in the whole book is in the footnotes, so why wouldn't you read them?

Conclusion of the Introduction

I think that's all I have to tell you for now. If you're the kind of person who reads introductions, thank you. If you're not, then you're probably not reading this so I don't know why I'm talking to you.

I hope that you enjoy this book. More importantly, I hope and pray that as you read it you will see more of the goodness of God and you are moved once again, or even for the first time, by his love for us in his son Jesus Christ.

"The sons of God went to the daughters of humans and had children by them." – Genesis 6:4

1

Angel Lovin'

Genesis 6:1-4

Hot Ladies and Angels

If you've ever wanted to sleep with an angel, don't. According to the Bible it's a pretty bad idea.

There was an advertisement on TV a few years ago for the deodorant brand Lynx (or Axe in some parts of the world). It featured angels falling from the sky, thumping into the ground inside an old Italian town. The angels – surprise, surprise – were very attractive woman-angels. They all started walking seductively from where they had landed through the streets of this town. The angels converged on one particular spot, where an average man was just getting off his scooter. He looked up in amazement to see the hot angels staring at him. They started to take their halos off and smash them on the ground. They were letting this guy know that they were willing to give up their holy status for him. Why? Well, we find out right at the end of the ad that it's because he's wearing Lynx. Lynx has such a good aroma angels can smell it from heaven, which means that either angels have an excellent sense of smell or Lynx is really pungent. You only have to hang with a bunch of teenage guys for a few minutes to know that it is most probably the latter.

Were you to show this ad to a bunch of Christians I suspect a good many of us would say, "Oh dear, how offensive! Angels would never do that. How dare you sully the name of angels!" I might be inclined to agree with that sentiment and be offended on behalf of angels everywhere, except that it's actually not outside the realm of possibility that heavenly creatures might want to sleep with humans. "That's absurd!" some might say. It's not. It's in the Bible! (To be fair things being absurd and being in the Bible are not mutually exclusive.)

This is what Genesis 6:1-4 says:

> When human beings began to increase in number on the earth and daughters were born to them, the sons of God saw that the daughters of humans were beautiful, and they married any of them they chose. Then the LORD said, "My Spirit will not contend with humans forever, for they are mortal; their days will be a hundred and twenty years."

> The Nephilim were on the earth in those days—and also afterward—when the sons of God went to the daughters of humans and had children by them. They were the heroes of old, men of renown.

Confused? Don't worry, you're not the first person. In fact, I've studied this passage quite a lot and I still feel a bit confused. We don't talk about this part of the Bible much in church because it's difficult for us, we're not exactly sure what is going on here.

Some people believe that spiritual beings and humans simply do not fraternise "in that way", so they try to find another explanation. Some people say this story is about the sons of Adam and Eve's third child, Seth, and the daughters of Cain who have met and had kids together. Just a bit of good old cousin marriage. Some people say that the story is about kings, who were sometimes referred to as sons of God, taking women for themselves and sleeping with them as was their royal prerogative.

Most biblical scholars, however, say that this is a story about angels sleeping with humans. Not everyone feels comfortable with this, but comfort aside, the scholars tend to accept that this is what the text says. The story seems to be that some male angels looked down from heaven, saw the good-looking human women walking around and thought, "Ooo baby, I gotta have some of that!" So they came down and convinced the women to marry them. "Check out these wings and these bright lights! Sexy time!"

When I was a young man I was often intimidated by those guys who were good looking, good at sport, could play guitar, and were just generally all-round good guys. I would despair in their company. I would wonder, "What hope do I have?" I suspect for the men who had to compete with the angels, they would have felt like I did, only much more acutely! How can any human man compare with an angel? If ever you feel outclassed for the affections of the one you love by some other prospective suitor or suitette (is that a word?), just be pleased you're not up against angels!

Once the angels managed to win the hand of the women, they proceeded to make angelic love to their new wives, who in due course popped out some literally cherubic babies. Don't ask too many questions about the biology of this. It's about as perplexing as the idea that Superman can father a human child. Just be assured that some human-angel babies were born. It'd be amazing if those babies grew up with supernatural abilities, for instance if they were able to fly, and had laser eyes or other such angel-baby upgrades, but it seems from this passage in Genesis that they just grew up to be giants called the Nephilim. Not that there is anything wrong with giants, but you have to admit, they're not as cool as powerful, human-angel hybrids with laser eyes.

Human-celestial-vampire-elven-orc romances might sound great to fantasy readers, but God, who has a particular way that he created things to be done, wasn't too fond of these human/angel fraternisations. He declared that from then on humans would only live for 120 years, and then he sent the flood.[1] God declared, "My Spirit will not contend with humans forever, for they are mortal; their days will be a hundred and twenty years" (v. 3). God was going to shorten the lifespan of humanity. No more of this living for almost a thousand years and thinking you can get away with anything. Nope, 120 years was all humans would now get. I suspect there were plenty of people disappointed that the round-the-world caravan trip they'd planned between the ages of 650-850 might not happen. Although there may be others, concerned they hadn't saved enough superannuation, who would be excited that they could just spend all that money that was meant to last them the 300 years after retirement. They could now just blow it all on stale crackers, mobility scooters, phone scams, and all those other things that old people seem fond of.[2]

---

1 If you're a super Bible nerd you may have worked out a problem. If this angel sexing led to the arrival of the Nephilim, but then the flood came, how did the Nephilim still appear after the flood (see Numbers 13:33)? Weren't they all dead? Did some of them stow away on the ark? Did they tread water for the entire flood? My wife suggested that because they are angel descendants they just hovered above the flood for the better part of a year till the waters receded. I think this is a silly idea but I told her I'd put it in the book. One possible explanation is that the angels took human lovers both before and after the flood, showing the depravity of humanity means they don't even care about the judgement of God. They sinned, God punished, God flooded, and then humans just got right on with more sinning. That may not be the answer, so keep thinking and praying, and let me know if you figure it out.

2 At this point some people may wonder how this 120-year sentence worked since Noah went on to live for 950 years, which is 730 years longer than allowed. Did Noah scam the system?

There are two possible explanations for this seeming disconnect

You may be asking, why would God punish humans for the sins of the angels? However, let me remind you that it takes two to tango. The angels may have come down for some good times, but it was the humans who married them. In those days women didn't really get much of a choice about who they married. They may have been the ones whom the angels married but it was their fathers who gave permission. This was a collaboration between the fathers and the angels. We don't get to see God dealing with angels (he may have given them some other unseen punishment), but what we do know is that humanity got the sentence of 120 years.

---

between what God says and what actually happens. One option is that Noah and all his friends were alive when God made the judgement. As a result the 120-year lifespan only applied to those born later. Like when the phone company puts up the price of phone plans they'll often only apply it to new contracts and leave everyone else on their old plans, which is how you find people using phones from the 90s paying $5 a month for twelve minutes worth of calls between the hours of 1 a.m. and 5 a.m. (these people are, coincidentally, usually the same people interested in eating stale crackers and drag-racing on mobility scooters). The new prices only kick in when you sign up for a new plan. It's like Noah and the others were on the old life plan and God slowly applied the new lifespan to the people born after his judgement. By the time of Moses people were only living for a maximum of 120 years (except Aaron, Moses' brother, who managed a respectable 123 years).

Another solution could be that actually what God was saying was not so much that humans would only live to 120 but that there would be 120 years from when God made the pronouncement to when God sent the flood. Thus people would only live 120 more years till they'd all be wiped out.

I keep changing my mind as to which explanation I like more. Perhaps the solution is in a mixture of the two.

So What Do Sexing Angels Have to Teach Us Today?

The question a passage like this obviously raises is, "What the heck are we meant to do with this?" How do you apply something like this to life in the twenty-first century?

The obvious takeaway from this passage is, don't date angels! I know sometimes a girl will fall in love with a boy and say something like, "Oh, he's an angel." Which is a perfectly reasonable thing to say, as long as it's only a metaphor. Before dating, or at very least, before marriage, be sure to check your future spouse for wings, a fiery sword, or a driver's licence with no clear date of birth. These are always dead giveaways that your new love is almost definitely an immortal spiritual being.

However, since most people in modern society are not in danger of dating a heavenly being, what else can we learn from this crazy story? The first thing we need to establish is why was God angry? Does God have a problem with giants? No. At least not as far as I know. I suspect God loves Hagrid even more than you or I do. The main problem of the story seems to be that humans and angels were conspiring to grant immortality to their offspring. The angels knew they had immortality; perhaps they were capable of passing that immortality on to their children. It's a weird passage, but this seems to be what God had a problem with.

In Genesis 3 Adam and Eve got kicked out of the Garden of Eden and their access to the Tree of Life, which grants everlasting life, was revoked. An angel with a wicked fire sword was to guard the entrance to the garden. I guess you could say the angel was guardin' the garden.

Without access to the Tree of Life, humans would now die. But then along came the angels with a scheme to help humans live forever and the humans jumped at the chance. The angels got sex, the humans got immortality, and everyone won - except God. God knows that it's his prerogative to give life and to take it away. No one, neither humans nor angels, has the right to take that role into their own hands.

Notice that God says, "My Spirit will not contend with humans forever, for they are mortal" (v. 3). God was saying that he was not going to share his life-giving power with people who are doomed to die. God breathed his Spirit into humanity to give us life, and he's not going to put up with people who think they can live without him. This is the problem that keeps popping up all throughout the Bible, and all throughout history: humanity thinks it can do whatever it wants without God. As much as we want to, we don't own life, we can't cheat death, and we can't exclude God.

Assumptions and the Fear of Death

How many movies or TV shows can you think of with immortal characters, or where people are trying to achieve immortality? You can probably think of a lot. I suspect this is because we don't really like death much, and the idea of living forever sounds pretty darn good.

In our society we're pretty uncomfortable with the idea of death. You may have noticed that on Instagram there are plenty of wedding photographers, plenty of birth photographers, but very few funeral photographers. Or, in fact, you may not have noticed because all you see on Instagram is memes and photos of your friends at the beach. Which makes sense because babies and weddings and memes and the beach are all much more fun than death. Death is depressing. Death is scary. No one wants to think about death.

But death is always lurking around.

Look at the way Western culture adores the young, and so many people aim to stay youthful with creams, plastic surgery, hair replacement, and Photoshop. Look at how rarely you see old people on TV, or in movies, and when you do they are nothing more than tropes (you know, people who love stale crackers, mobility scooters, and phone scams, that kind of trope). We don't often treat them as valuable members of our community, full of hard-won experience and wisdom for us to draw on. Imagine if we did value old people the way we value the young. Our YouTube stars wouldn't just be young people giving us beauty tips and doing dumb pranks (though I need beauty tips and I love videos of people hurting themselves), they would also be octogenarians telling us about inner beauty and the things they learned from the dumb pranks they pulled when they were younger.

I think all this obsession with youth and beauty might be because we are afraid of death. Elderly people show us where

9

we're headed and we don't want to be reminded that one day we will be like them and that one day we will die too.

When I was young a famous scientist from TV came to my school and told us all that science is getting so good, soon we'd be able to live forever, soon we could beat death. He said that in the near future we would simply grow ourselves new limbs and new organs to replace any part that didn't work. This all sounds good in theory but there are certainly plenty of questions about the ethical shortcuts we might be taking to get there. If you've ever seen *The Island* starring Scarlett Johansson and Obi Wan Kenobi you'll know what I'm talking about.

One of the challenges of these verses in Genesis 6 is that they ask us to think about our assumptions about both life and death. The humans and the angels seem to think that beating death is the ideal state. They want to live forever, to contend with God for eternity, but what if living forever isn't all it's cracked up to be?

Of course, there is the obvious problem that immortal people have that all the people they love get flabby and die while they stay young and beautiful for eternity. But maybe there is also a very important reason why God stopped humanity from eating from the Tree of Life. What if God wasn't just working out his judgement, but also protecting humanity from living forever in a broken, sinful world?

When I'm on holidays, sleeping in, eating good food, and the weather is great, I want to live forever. I imagine spending all time travelling the world, to all the most beautiful locations, eating the best potato dishes the world has offer. But when I'm confronted with all the pain and sadness of this world, I can't imagine having to put up with it for eternity. The violence, the sin, the sickness, and distress – how much of this can we endure? Perhaps death is a part of God's mercy.

This thought should give us pause. If our desire to live forever is misplaced, then what else have we got wrong? What other assumptions about life and death might we have accepted without questioning?

Challenging our assumptions should cause us to ask lots of tricky questions, seeking answers that might be different from what we expect. What might be God's view of the life of an unborn child? Does the Bible have any wisdom for us when we think about medically prolonging life beyond its natural term? When can humans ethically create life? When can we ethically take life?

These are all big questions. Questions too big for the scope of this book. Were we to pursue them we might never make it to all the wonderful stories about nudity, farts, and zombies ahead, and that would be pretty disappointing. But that doesn't mean they aren't worth asking, even if you think they're too big for you. Big questions are important questions, and asking them seriously and humbly shows that we are aiming to tread lightly, to not make assumptions lest we repeat the sins of our ancestors and their angel lovers.

Jesus and the Death of Death

All this thinking about life and death is pretty difficult stuff to deal with. But there is light in all this, there is Jesus. While in this story we have seen humans and angels seeking immortality by taking what is God's for themselves, in Jesus Christ we see God becoming mortal and giving up his rights and privileges as God, for our sake. While we grasp for the divine, seeking to usurp God, Jesus Christ "did not consider equality with God something to be used to his own advantage; rather, he made himself nothing" (Philippians 2:6-7). Through Jesus' incarnation (that is, God becoming human) and through his death on the cross, Jesus secured for humanity eternal life, the very thing that we want, but cannot gain on our own. When Jesus rose from the dead he showed that the outcome of death can be life for all who would trust in him. In his resurrection we discover what true life without end looks like. It is not a stolen immortality in a decaying world, but a new body that will never get sick or die, living forever in a new, remade creation. Look at these words of Paul about what our resurrection bodies will be like:

> Listen, I tell you a mystery: We will not all sleep, but we will all be changed—in a flash, in the twinkling of an eye, at the last trumpet. For the trumpet will sound, the dead will be raised imperishable, and we will be changed. For the perishable must clothe itself with the imperishable, and the mortal with immortality. When the perishable has been clothed with the imperishable, and the mortal with

immortality, then the saying that is written will come true: "Death has been swallowed up in victory." (1 Corinthians 15:51-54)

What a great hope we have to look forward to!

In Genesis 6 the sin of humanity means human life is shortened. In the obedience of Jesus, he receives our punishment, and we receive life – life forever! It turns out the road to immortality is not through the angels, but through the cross.

"[Noah] became drunk and lay uncovered inside his tent." – Genesis 9:21

2

Drunk Noah's Post-Cruise Party

Genesis 9:18-29

Noah's Ark is not a Kids' Story

Noah! What a guy! Builder of Boats, Friend to the Animals, Sailor of the High Seas of God's Terrible Judgement. There's something about the story of Noah that people love to tell to kids. The story gets taught in Sunday School, sung about in songs, painted in murals, and made into happy cartoons. When I was a kid my next door neighbour even had it printed on the curtains in his bedroom. However, when you look carefully at the story of Noah's ark, it's clear that it's not really a good story for kids. At first glance it sounds nice enough: it's got a boat and some animals, both things that kids tend to like. What they generally aren't so keen on is the drowning of a planet's entire human population save one family. That's not cheery stuff. I doubt my neighbour would have been too pleased with pictures of people falling to their watery graves haunting his first and last waking moments of each day. But we tend not to think about that. We just think about the animals, because animals are cute – especially when they're all coupled up.

When you read the story it's clear that Noah's ark is not for kids, no matter how good a giraffe may look with its neck sticking out the top window of a boat (and they do look pretty good). It's about God's judgement on a violent and sinful world. The people who think Noah's ark is a kids' story are probably the same ones who love to teach kids about Samson – you know, that happy-go-lucky guy who killed 1000 men with a donkey's jawbone. What fun times!

All that said, in this chapter we're not actually looking at the story of Noah's ark, because it's not that funny. Giraffes are funny. Mass drownings are not. Not even to me. What *is* funny is what happens after Noah gets off the ark. The actual fun bit, that everyone leaves out, contains drunkenness, peeping Toms, and 600-year-old genitals. That is fun for the whole family!

The One Where Noah Gets Drunk and Naked

The story begins after Noah has gotten off the boat, made a covenant with God, seen a rainbow, and all that beautiful symbolic stuff. And Noah, it seems, really needed a drink. I'm not much of a drinker, but I can imagine after spending over a year on a boat with just your family and a bunch of copulating animals (why else do you think there were two of each animal – conversation?) I would want a drink too.

> Noah, a man of the soil, proceeded to plant a vineyard. When he drank some of its wine, he became drunk and lay uncovered inside his tent. (Genesis 9:20-21)

For Noah to get a drink he didn't just wander down to the bottle shop, or the pub and grab a beer. Noah had to plant a vineyard, grow the vines, harvest the grapes, squash them, ferment them, bottle them (or wine skin them probably) and then finally he was ready to have his drink. That would have taken years. Noah was a man committed to his drink, so when the wine finally arrived he didn't hold back. The Bible is very politely saying that Noah got totally smashed, sang some bad karaoke, tried to fight the bouncers, told everyone he loved them, fell off his barstool, then went home and fell asleep naked. That's not ideal behaviour by anyone but it's particularly bad for a guy who was considered to be a "righteous man" (Genesis 6:9). And what should have happened next was that Noah woke up with a splitting headache and smelling faintly of vomit, scrolled through the previous night's texts, phone calls, and social media posts to piece together a sequence of events and issue apologies where necessary, swore he would never have another drink, and then proceeded to never talk about that night again. Except that's not what happened:

> Ham, the father of Canaan, saw his father naked and told his
> two brothers outside. (Genesis 9:22)

Ham went to visit his dad's tent. When he walked in and saw Noah naked, he ran to tell his brothers, which is a very weird thing to do. That's like kissing-your-sibling weird.

No one wants to see their dad naked. It's the kind of thing normal people work pretty hard to avoid. And if you do accidentally see your dad's bits you don't run out and tell everyone. You don't jump on Facebook and announce, "Just saw my dad naked! Laugh reacts only!" You block it out of your memory and try to move on.

Ham, on the other hand, thought it was awesome. He ran out to tell his brothers. "Hey guys, come here! I just saw dad's dong!" Keep in mind that Noah was 600 years old. I can't even begin to imagine what a naked 600-year-old man looks like (though, to be honest, I haven't tried very hard). The state of the package didn't seem to bother Ham at all though – he was happy to invite his brothers to share his discovery. Noah should be pleased there was no Instagram back then. No matter how many filters you slap over it, 600-year-old junk doesn't look good at any time.

Ham's brothers responded a little better than Ham. Brothers do tend to get up to mischief, but this was one step too far for them. So Shem and Japheth did things a little more like you and I might:

But Shem and Japheth took a garment and laid it across
their shoulders; then they walked in backward and covered
their father's naked body. Their faces were turned the other
way so that they would not see their father naked.
(Genesis 9:23)

Shem and Japheth took some kind of garment (a rug, a poncho,
a raincoat – I assume they had a few of them around), hung
it across their shoulders, then wisely walked in backwards
so they didn't see their dad's wedding equipment. Probably
because they were worried they'd be struck blind, or at the
very least have to spend years in therapy, and therapy hadn't
even been invented yet.

When Noah awoke from his wine and found out what his
youngest son had done to him, he said,

"Cursed be Canaan!
The lowest of slaves
will he be to his brothers."

He also said,

"Praise be to the LORD, the God of Shem!
May Canaan be the slave of Shem.
May God extend Japheth's territory;
may Japheth live in the tents of Shem,
and may Canaan be the slave of Japheth."

> After the flood Noah lived 350 years. Noah lived a total of
> 950 years, and then he died. (Genesis 9:24-29)

When Noah woke up, not only did he have a killer hangover he somehow found out what Ham had done and he was angry. Noah may have been funny when he was drunk but he was definitely not funny the next day. Noah cursed Ham, and his kids (who became the Canaanites), for how he treated his dad.

That may seem a bit extreme to us. What Ham did may have been immature, but it wasn't evil, was it? All he did was try to share something amusing with his brothers. However, this is not just about an immature son. The Bible is clear that honouring your parents is very important, it's even one of the Ten Commandments (see Exodus 20:12). The Ten Commandments are about loving God and loving others. To disrespect your father both dishonours the relationship and hurts the man. Ham hadn't just had a laugh, he had attacked his own sacred relationship with his father. As a consequence of his actions, he and his children were cursed by Noah.

However, it may be worth noting that Noah's curse did not come from God. The curse may indicate the gravity of the sin, but it doesn't mean that God had cursed Ham. Noah is the same guy who got drunk and fell asleep naked a few verses earlier. Noah's curse could be a godly curse, but he could also have been acting out of his own sinfulness and wounded pride.

Whatever the case, whether this curse and Shem and Japheth's blessings are honoured by God or not, they have been included in the Bible so we cannot just discount them as the irrelevant rantings of an embarrassed, hungover man. We need to remember that what can seem like a bit of fun in the moment can have lasting consequences for our relationships with those around us. And what seems like a small act of goodness (carrying a blanket is not hard work) can have lasting positive repercussions. Our actions, good and bad, reverberate throughout our lives and the lives of those around us.

When you first read this story you may have thought God put it in the Bible just because naked old men are funny, but hopefully it's becoming clear that there is more to this than just a few willy jokes, and we're not done yet . . .

Parents Can Be Dumb, But That Doesn't Mean You Should Be

Noah was probably a pretty good guy. I suspect his kids were generally pleased with him as a dad. He did build a giant boat to save them and their families and subsequently provide a floating petting zoo for his grandkids. It'd be hard not to respect a dad who did that.

Sadly even the best of parents will do dumb things. Chances are, if you think carefully, you can remember one or two things your parents have done that they wouldn't be entirely proud of. It's a sad day when you realise your parents aren't perfect.

One question this story raises for us is, how will we treat our parents when they don't act in a manner worthy of respect?

Some of us have great parents, some of us have rubbish parents. All of us have to choose how we will treat our parents despite how they behave. We can choose to be like Ham, to mock our parents, to use their mistakes for our own amusement, or for future ammunition. Or we can choose to honour our parents, to not hold their mistakes against them, to cover over their mistakes despite how we might want to respond.

The parent-child relationship is perhaps the most basic of all relationships. Our parents are the people we may have the strongest feelings about. They are the people whom we love first and the people who can invoke feelings of greatest warmth and greatest frustration. They can make us feel safe or they can cause our deepest wounds. Because of this sometimes it is in our relationship with our parents that we can find it hardest to be the people we want to be. The challenge of this story is to always honour our parents no matter how dishonourable their behaviour. If we can do this perhaps when they come to their senses they will look back at how we cared for them and know we honoured them, even if they didn't deserve it.

The Bible shows us that we have a loving Father in heaven who loves us even when we don't deserve it. He has covered over our sin instead of publicly shaming us. We can ask God to help us to have love for our parents that flows out of his love for us and our love for him. We can honour them, because he has honoured us.

None of this means that if our parents are abusive and hurtful that we must just put up with it. Love and honour never mean we have to put up with sin, dismiss it, or cannot seek help to deal with it. Love and honour mean that even as we might put firm boundaries in place in unhealthy relationships we treat those who hurt us with dignity and respect, never dehumanising them or ignoring that they were also created in the image of God, despite how they might have treated us and others.

Ham dehumanised his father by using him for a laugh. Shem and Japheth recognised their father's sin, and sought to protect him as he had protected them. Honouring our parents means honouring them even when they are acting dishonourably, for when we do this we honour our Father in heaven.

Drunk People are not Fair Game

When we look at this story we can learn not just how we deal with parents but how we deal with drinking and drunkenness. You can be told over and over again not to get drunk (see Proverbs 20:1, Galatians 5:19-21, Ephesians 5:18) but often it's not until you see the effects of drunkenness that you actually learn something. Just hearing a lecture on not getting drunk is rarely going to stop someone from drinking to excess, but I've regularly heard people say things like, "I'm never drinking again" in the aftermath of drinking too much. Here the Bible offers the perfect opportunity to learn from the mistakes of others. Let Noah's bender and subsequent embarrassment save you the hassle of doing it yourself.

However, perhaps a more pressing lesson to learn from this story is that drunk people are not fair game. Ham saw his father's nakedness and thought he could use his dad's inebriation for his own pleasure. Drunk people are not for our personal pleasure. This is a lesson we badly need to learn. It is estimated that alcohol is a factor in half of all sexual assaults. In one study of university students, 30% of people surveyed said that they had experienced "alcohol-related non-consensual sex". In another study of victims of sexual assault "approximately 37% of respondents reported that their perpetrator had consumed alcohol either on its own or in conjunction with other substances prior to the assault"[1]. It is clear that many people use drunkenness as a chance to get what they want out of other people, either because of the victim's increased vulnerability or their own decreased inhibitions. While we can't say alcohol is to blame for sexual assault, it does exacerbate our already broken relationships, views about sex, and willingness to use others to our own advantage.

---

1   Figures quoted in L. Wall & A. Quadara, *Under the influence? Considering the role of alcohol and sexual assault in social contexts (ACSSA Issue No. 18)*, Melbourne: Australian Centre for the Study of Sexual Assault, Australian Institute of Family Studies, 2014. It should be noted that the study makes clear that due to the different terms of what is being assessed in the studies, differing ways in which alcohol consumption is defined and different populations across the studies "it is difficult to know what to make of the findings." The paper concludes that in regards to sexual assault, "The research clarifies that [alcohol consumption] is, on its own, not a single causative factor, but that cognitive and pharmacological effects of alcohol intersect with other aspects of victim and perpetrator characteristics and personality traits, beliefs about sex and alcohol, and social and cultural norms or scripts around gender and alcohol." Sorry, that wasn't a very fun footnote.

When Ham takes advantage of his father, Noah's anger is justified. Noah is vulnerable and Ham used him for his own fun. Ham turned Noah's drunkenness into an opportunity to dehumanise his father – treating him as merely a source of amusement for himself and his brothers. Now I'm not insinuating that Ham took sexual advantage of his father (although some Bible scholars have suggested that's not beyond the realm of interpretive possibility), but even without the possibility of sexual abuse, Ham turning his father's nakedness into a joke is a self-serving, dishonouring act.

It's Shem and Japheth who give us an example of how to respond to the vulnerable person. Shem and Japheth, far from seeing their father's nakedness as an opportunity for a laugh, choose to act to restore his dignity and preserve his honour. When they cover their father's nakedness and refuse to look at him, it's not because the sight of a naked 600 year old is unpleasant (though surely it is, all those wrinkles) but because they refuse to dehumanise him and disrespect him. He is their father, the one they honour. He is not their joke, their source of fun, or their object to toy with.

Likewise, when we come across people who are drunk, our job is to treat them with dignity and respect. For guys this means a woman's drunkenness is never a chance for you to take advantage of her. Regardless of what kind of sexual activity you think is appropriate for your situation[2] and whether or

---

2 According to the Bible we should be saving sex for marriage, though I suspect not everyone is going to agree with this. But no matter what your thoughts are on when it's appropriate to do what sexually, it's

not you think she'd consent were she sober, a drunk person is not there for you to have your way with. While she does not have the capacity to make rational decisions she cannot give consent, and it is an attack on her rights for you to use her to get your thrills, whether that is to kiss her or to go as far as having sex with her. At best you're taking advantage of her, at worst you're committing sexual assault and rape.

For girls the principle is the same. You should never take advantage of drunk guys. They are not your playthings. They are people loved by God just as you are. Your job is to treat them as you would like to be treated yourself.

But this is not just confined to the area of sex. When people are drunk you can get them to do all sorts of things. You might think it's funny to convince them to do more shots, dance on a table, ride in a shopping trolley, jump off a balcony, or surf on the top of a bus, but when a person doesn't have the mental faculties to make rational decisions, you're using their drunkenness as an opportunity to exercise power over them. By all means do dumb stuff with your friends – dance in public, sing bad karaoke, race shopping trolleys, order pizza at 3 a.m. – this passage isn't telling us not to have fun. It is teaching us not to take advantage of drunk people.

So how can we be more like Shem and Japheth? When we find ourselves hanging out with drunk people, we treat them how

---

never appropriate to take advantage of someone with limited mental and/or physical capacities.

we would like to be treated. When everyone else is telling them to do something stupid, you can tell them they don't have to. When someone is doing something "hilarious" you can be the one person not pulling out your phone to record it for social media. When they're feeling amorous and trying to kiss you, you can gently tell them you'll consider their very flattering affections if they're still interested once they've sobered up. When they're stumbling around you can help them get home safely. When someone is trying to take advantage of them, you can protect them. When they've vomited on their clothes, you can find them clean ones. When they want to drink more, you can encourage them to have a Coke instead. And when you get sent photos and videos of people doing embarrassing things while drunk, don't look at them, or go searching for them, and don't pass them on.

Of course, we shouldn't be getting drunk, but we also need to care for those who are drunk. Inebriated people are vulnerable people, vulnerable to their own stupidity and vulnerable to others' malicious intent. You have the opportunity to protect and care. Stay sober, and love, honour, and help those who aren't. It's the Shem and Japheth way.

Jesus

One more thing we can learn from this story of Noah's nude nap is about the greatness of Jesus. When we look at the bigger picture of what's going on we see that even though God had decided to destroy the earth because it was "corrupt in God's sight and full of violence" (Genesis 6:11), he decided not to destroy all humanity but to save a remnant through Noah and the ark that he would build.

Noah built the ark and he and his family were saved. When the flood receded and they all got off the ark, God made a covenant with Noah and his family never to flood the earth again, and he commanded them to "Be fruitful and increase in number and fill the earth" (Genesis 9:1), just like he did with Adam and Eve (see Genesis 1:28). God was starting again with Noah and his family. Things went bad the first time, but God had saved a few and would begin a new humanity through Noah.

You would expect everyone to live happily ever after, wouldn't you? This was a chance for everyone to start over, to renounce the corrupt and wicked ways of old, and build a new earth for everyone. Everyone should have just got to work building a community of love, harmony, and rainbows.

But what happens? Noah gets trashed, falls asleep naked, and his son takes advantage of him. So much for a new humanity. The wickedness hasn't been killed off. It stowed away on the boat in the hearts of Noah and his family.

God is showing us that this world will not be fixed by wiping everything out and starting again. You can't start a new humanity with the same old material. We need something better.

And so Jesus comes along. And, like Noah, God decides to use him to save those he has chosen from his coming wrath. Yet this time God saves not through an ark, but through the body of Christ, beaten and crucified to account for the sins of the world. Those who wish to be saved look not to a wooden boat, but to a rugged cross.

While Noah and his family emerged from their ark as the same people in a world wiped out, Jesus emerged from his tomb, with a new body, with death wiped out. God promised to start a new humanity in Jesus. Jesus, unlike Noah, has a pure heart and he promises a new heart to all who put their faith in him. The wickedness of this world is put to death in us as we look to Jesus, and one day it will be totally wiped clean when Jesus returns to establish the new creation and give us new eternal bodies. This is the new covenant – God's new way of relating to the world.

When Noah and his family are saved through Noah's ark, we are pointed to the cross that saves us from the coming wrath of God. When Noah fails to live up to the new covenant as head of the new humanity we look to Christ – our head of the new humanity who has not, cannot and will not fail. Once and for all sin is defeated, judgement is quenched, and death will be done away with. Noah points us to the better promise of Jesus Christ.

What great news! We might fail, we might get drunk and fall asleep naked, we might take advantage of those who are vulnerable, and we might struggle to put right the wrongs of this world. But when we put our trust in Jesus, he is the one who is standing beside us, forgiving us for our corruption and sin, and working with us as we honour and care for those around us, whatever state they may be in.

"When the donkey saw the angel of the Lord standing in the road with a drawn sword in his hand, it turned off the road into a field." – Numbers 22:23

3

Balaam's Talking Ass

Numbers 22:21-41

When discussing crazy stories in the Bible, this is probably the gold standard. This is the only time in recorded history when a donkey talks.[1] We have talking parrots, howling dogs, cats on YouTube who can play piano, and goats who sing Taylor Swift, but outside of fictional stories and *Shrek*, there aren't any talking donkeys. That makes this passage a prime piece of Scripture for our detailed theological analysis.

A Man, a Donkey, and an Angel Walk Into a Ravine . . .

The story takes place after Israel has made it out of Egypt. They'd been wandering about in the desert grumbling for about forty years but eventually made it to the edge of the

---

1 I assume this is true, I haven't actually bothered to read all of recorded history looking for talking donkeys.

Promised Land. As they travelled they kept getting into fights with locals, and winning. They arrived in the territory of Moab, and Moab's king, Balak, started getting nervous. He was afraid that the Israelites were going to be trouble. He said, "This horde is going to lick up everything around us, as an ox licks up the grass of the field" (Numbers 22:4). I assume this licking that the Israelites were going to do would involve swords and pillaging rather than actual licking, as that's not all that threatening. Except, perhaps, to one's hygiene.

Balak's fear of Israel's powerful, military-grade tongues caused him to turn to a famous diviner named Balaam whom he thought might be able to put a curse on the Israelites. He sent some of his elders with Balaam's normal divination fee and this message:

> A people has come out of Egypt; they cover the face of
> the land and have settled next to me. Now come and put a
> curse on these people, because they are too powerful for
> me. Perhaps then I will be able to defeat them and drive
> them out of the land. For I know that whoever you bless is
> blessed, and whoever you curse is cursed. (vv. 5-6)

Balaam knew that if he was going to curse the Israelites he would have to deal with their God, Yahweh. So he said, "Stay here, I'll have a chat to Yahweh and let you know what we can sort out."

That night, instead of Balaam summoning God, God turned up to Balaam and asked, "Who are these men with you?" (v. 9).

Balaam explained what Balak asked of him in great detail, as if God didn't already know (vv. 10-11). It was like one of those prayers you hear in church sometimes: "God, as you know we're having a bake sale on Sunday 17th August at 5 p.m. in the Jezebel McPastry Memorial Hall, which has just recently been renovated. We're hoping to raise money for our youth group trip to the beach in the first week of January. We need to raise at least $500 to cover the bus hire and tinned spaghetti for our beach games, which are going to be awesome. So please help us to raise the money. And please let there be enough people contributing cakes and other baked goods, and one or two people who are willing to volunteer after the service to make some gluten-free and dairy-free cakes for those among us who have digestive issues, that would be a wonderful answer to prayer. Amen." But I digress . . .

So, Balaam explained what Balak had asked of him, and God, in his infinite patience, didn't respond, "Yes, I know all this, get to the point." He said, "Do not go with them. You must not put a curse on those people, because they are blessed" (v. 12).

This seems like a pretty clear answer: "Don't go. Don't curse. They're blessed."

Balaam went back to the officials and told them he couldn't do it because God said he can't. They returned to Balak with the bad news, but Balak wouldn't take "No" for an answer. He sent more officials, and more important officials. If the last time he sent the Deputy Director of Curse Acquirement, the next time he sent the Director of Curse Acquirement, and the Minister for Blessings and Curses, as well as the Royal Taskforce for Dangerous Licking Prevention. They came with all the pomp they could muster and a bunch more money.

Balaam said, "Even if Balak gave me all the silver and gold in his palace, I could not do anything great or small to go beyond the command of the LORD my God. Now spend the night here so that I can find out what else the LORD will tell me" (vv. 18-19).

He was essentially saying, "I can't. I can't . . . No, I couldn't possibly take your money. God said, 'No'. He said, 'No!' . . . But let me just check . . . I'll check if he has something else that he might like to add. How much money are you offering again? Oh that's too much . . . Let me just check."

I suspect he was hoping God would change his mind and Balaam would get a big chunk of change - after all, this was how he made his bread and butter. God's "No" was clear the first time, but Balaam was hoping he wouldn't have to take "No" for an answer.

Knowing Balaam's heart, God let Balaam go, but told him "do only what I tell you" (v. 20).

Probably Balaam heard this and just thought, "Dollar, dollar bills, y'all!" and went off to pack his bags, leaving plenty of room for the cash.

In the morning Balaam got on his donkey so he could visit Balak and start making some sweet curse coin. However, God was very angry. As Balaam and his donkey were travelling along, the donkey saw the angel standing there with his sword out, ready to destroy Balaam, and she[2] veered off the path to save him from an angel stabbing. Not knowing what the donkey was doing, Balaam got angry and beat her. Further along, they were walking down a narrow path with walls on each side. The angel turned up again, and again the donkey tried to avoid the angel by walking around him. In the process Balaam got his foot crushed against the wall. This made him even angrier and he beat the donkey a second time. A third time they were walking along when the angel turned up. This time the road was so narrow the donkey couldn't get past the angel at all, so she just sat down. Balaam was furious and beat the donkey with his staff.

Suddenly God gave the donkey the gift of tongues and she turned to Balaam and spoke to him. She said, "What have I done to you to make you beat me these three times?" (v. 28).

To which Balaam replied, "You have made a fool of me! If only I had a sword in my hand, I would kill you right now" (v. 29). Which is amazing! Why is his first response not "Ahh! A talking donkey!"?[3] How often did Balaam encounter talking donkeys? Did he know Donkey from *Shrek*? Was he friends with Mr Ed?

---

2   If you're wondering why the donkey is a "she" and not an "it", it's because in the Hebrew the word for donkey indicates that she's a female donkey. Seeing as she's a sassy, back-talking donkey, I thought she deserved to be a "she" here too.

3   Incidentally, my wife's favourite joke goes like this: Two muffins are sitting in an oven. One turns to the other and says, "Wow! It's hot in here!" and the other responds, "Ahh! A talking muffin!"

How could he be so chill in the face of a chatty ass? Probably Balaam was so angry with the donkey that he didn't even stop to think about the fact she was talking to him. We've all shouted at inanimate objects before when they don't work the way we want them to, and maybe we've been in such a rage that we wouldn't even be surprised if they talked back. I guess this was the ancient equivalent of techno rage. The donkey was just like Siri having a go at us when we get stroppy with her.

The donkey decided to reason with Balaam because it makes a lot of sense to reason with a man talking to a donkey. She said, "Am I not your own donkey, which you have always ridden, to this day? Have I been in the habit of doing this to you?" (v. 30).

"No," sulked Balaam.

Then God opened Balaam's eyes and he could see, standing there, sword drawn, the angel of the Lord! He'd been there the whole time and only then did Balaam see him. Balaam fell on his face, hoping not to get destroyed.

The angel stuck up for the donkey, saying, "Why have you beaten your donkey these three times? I have come here to oppose you because your path is a reckless one before me. The donkey saw me and turned away from me these three times. If it had not turned away, I would certainly have killed you by now, but I would have spared it" (vv. 32-33).

I suspect that the angel was being kind to the donkey here. He implied that the donkey saved Balaam's life. But if the angel really wanted to kill Balaam he could have done it. It's not as if the donkey could outwit or outrun the angel. Donkeys are great but they've got nothing on an angel, especially not when you consider that in one night this very angel slaughted 185,000 people (see 2 Kings 19:35). This angel has some serious skills.

Balaam, being a bit of a twit, said, "I have sinned. I did not realise you were standing in the road to oppose me. Now if you are displeased, I will go back" (v. 34).

What did he mean, "If you are displeased"? Of course the angel was displeased! He was standing there with his sword out ready to kill him because of Balaam's reckless path. How much more evidence did Balaam need of the angel's displeasure! The angel ignored one of the biggest understatements of the Bible[4] and allowed him to go, but told him the same instructions God gave Balaam before: "speak only what I tell you" (v. 35).

So off Balaam went. When he arrived to meet Balak, Balak berated him for taking so long. Balaam could at this point have said, "Look, I'm sorry I'm late but I was almost killed by an angel and was only just saved by my talking donkey. It's been a big day, can you cut me some slack?"

---

4 For the greatest understatement of the New Testament read Luke 4:2 where it describes Jesus' forty-day fast in the desert then says, "He ate nothing during those days, and at the end of them he was hungry." I get hungry if I skip lunch, I don't know what I'd be if I didn't eat for forty days but it'd certainly be more of a situation than merely "hungry".

But he merely said, "Well, I have come to you now. But I can't say whatever I please. I must speak only what God puts in my mouth" (v. 38).

In the end Balaam blessed Israel and cursed their enemies, much to the distress of Balak who refused to pay him any money. God turned Israel's curses into blessings and Balaam went home empty handed, but with a great story to tell his kids.

Why So Angry, God?

It's easy when reading this story to get a little outraged about God sending an angel to kill Balaam right after he was given permission to go. Why would he do this? Is God fickle? Does he just enjoy toying with Balaam? Hopefully I've foreshadowed the answer to this question above in my exceptionally good retelling of the story. However, if you missed the answer, let me give it to you straight.

Balaam was a greedy man. He was a diviner who practised witchcraft for money. And when Balak's delegation came asking him to pronounce a curse on Israel and Yahweh said "No", that should have been the end of it. But it wasn't the end of it. Balaam was willing to go back to God, hoping the answer would change, hoping he'd pick up some dosh. We know Balaam was greedy because that's what we're told in later parts of the Bible. In 2 Peter 2:14-16 Peter says this about some false teachers who are attacking the church:

> With eyes full of adultery, they never stop sinning; they
> seduce the unstable; they are experts in greed—an accursed
> brood! They have left the straight way and wandered off to
> follow the way of Balaam son of Bezer, who loved the wages
> of wickedness. But he was rebuked for his wrongdoing by
> a donkey—an animal without speech—who spoke with a
> human voice and restrained the prophet's madness.

Then Jude verse 11, referring to people who are polluting the church, says this:

> Woe to them! They have taken the way of Cain; they
> have rushed for profit into Balaam's error; they have been
> destroyed in Korah's rebellion.

Balaam, as one witty Internet article puts it, was a prophet for profit. God let him go, so he could meet him on the road and oppose him, making clear to Balaam that he was not at liberty to say whatever paid the best; he was free only to say what God allowed him to say.

What's interesting is that while in the story it looks like Balaam is just a bit of a greedy bumbler, every mention we get of Balaam in the rest of the Bible is wholly negative. Later in Numbers Balaam gets killed when the Israelites fight with the Midianites (see Numbers 31:7-8). We also read about how the Midianite women had followed Balaam's advice and tried to entice the Israelites to sin (see Numbers 31:15-16). Throughout the rest of the Old Testament whenever Balaam is mentioned it is to show how Balak had hired Balaam to curse Israel, but

God would not listen to the curse. Balaam is a picture of a prophet for hire: he wasn't interested in what God wanted, he just wanted to make a quick buck.

Letting God Set the Agenda

The first challenge of this passage is to make sure we let God set the agenda. In the story, Balaam could only bless what God blessed and curse what God cursed – he was ruled by God's agenda under the fear of death. For you and me, God usually allows us more freedom. We get to choose what we participate in, what we love, what we hate, and what we speak for, and what we speak against. As far as it is possible we need to make sure our values line up with God's values, that we love the things God loves and we hate the things God hates. Too often, our values and our behaviour are not dictated by the heart of God, but by the culture we live in. How we treat others, how we view those who are different from ourselves, how we spend our time and money, all of it can be the product of our culture and surroundings. We have to make sure that God's values take priority, by knowing his will and obeying it. How do we know God's will? We find it in his Word, and we'll learn it as we spend time with his people. Studying God's Word and seeking to understand it and live it out with others will help us better understand God's will for our lives and for the world.

Letting God set the agenda may cost us. It certainly cost Balaam all his pay, and we know he loved his pay. When we love what God loves and hate what God hates, we may lose friends who disagree with us. We may not be able to keep doing things we love doing if we realise that God hates it. We may find ourselves unable to do things in our jobs or with our friends that might compromise our ethics or that turn out not to be so loving. There are rewards though too. As we invest in the things God loves, we will find ourselves building his kingdom, which is the only thing that lasts. We will find we have opportunities to love people and care for them that we hadn't anticipated. We'll have the deep satisfaction of knowing that we're living a life that matches God's values.

The problem with all this is that it can be terribly difficult. But just as the angel told Balaam to "speak only what I tell you" (Numbers 22:35), implying God's continued presence, we have God with us, speaking to us, and empowering us. Jesus promised his Holy Spirit would be with us (see John 14:15-21). We have God's presence, on our side, helping us to stand strong and not to give in like Balaam, but to live lives which honour God, letting him set the agenda. We can be people with greater conviction and faithfulness than the prophet who got rebuked by a donkey.

The Message and the Messenger

The second challenge of this passage is in how we relate to those who bring us God's message. When Balaam did speak, after his donkey incident, he didn't actually curse Israel. He was unable to curse Israel because in the end he worked for God. In the end everyone works for God. Even a donkey speaks for God if that is what God wants. This means that just because a message is good, it doesn't mean the messenger is any good. The message doesn't validate the messenger.

Balaam said some amazing things in Numbers 23-24 but he was not a great prophet. He couldn't even see the angel of the Lord that was standing right in front of him. His donkey had better spiritual eyesight than him. Yet Balaam was compelled by God to say exactly what God wanted him to say. The message doesn't validate the messenger nor does the messenger validate the message. This is important to remember because once you get stuck into the Christian life you hear a lot of messages from a lot of messengers. Sometimes we can find a preacher we love, and then they can get caught in some sin or scandal and we find ourselves questioning everything they ever said.

Once there was a man who was getting quite a bit of fame around Christian circles. He was suffering from a deadly disease, and he would travel around to speak and minister to large crowds who were inspired by his faith in the face of terrible sickness. Unfortunately, it transpired that he had made up the entire ordeal to hide a sin he was ashamed of. There were some kids in my youth group who had been particularly affected by his story and teaching and when the truth came out they were understandably hurt and confused. I spoke to them at the time about how sometimes the people we look to as spiritual leaders can let us down, but that doesn't invalidate the message they shared. The Jesus they point us to is still faithful – he is just, good, and loving whether or not the people who speak on his behalf are good and faithful or not.[5]

---

5 At least I hope I said something like that. I like to hope I'm as inspiring in real life as I am in my memories. Chances are I tried to say something inspiring and ended up saying, "Cheer up mate, Jesus is the goodest" and then went off to play some game involving marshmallows.

If God can speak through a greedy prophet and an everyday donkey, then he can speak through anyone. This means that your favourite preacher, pastor, youth leader, songwriter, or mentor may say some great things, but that doesn't mean that they aren't sinners too. In some cases they may not even believe what they're saying, but that doesn't make it untrue. God can speak the truth through donkeys and through liars - he can speak through anyone.

On the flipside, the messenger doesn't validate the message. Balaam was able to preach both lies and truth. He was pretty popular with Balak and his crew, but most of what he said were just the words he was paid to say. Sometimes the most kind, friendly, and charismatic people can preach lies. Just because you like a person doesn't mean everything they say is true.

I remember one day listening to a man preach who was a missionary and had been doing extraordinary things overseas, with many people coming to faith in Jesus. He was a pretty impressive guy whose life was clearly committed to Jesus, and when I'd met him previously he'd been kind and sincere. But as I listened to him preach that day I started to get uncomfortable about some of the things he said. I particularly remember him saying, "You're not a Christian until you've brought someone else to faith." Now I know the reasons behind why he said what he said; he was passionate about people hearing about Jesus and he was sick of Christians who aren't interested in sharing the best news they have ever heard. However, when you read the Bible it's pretty clear that you are a Christian when you put your faith in Jesus as Lord and Saviour – nothing more, nothing less. This guy was a passionate servant of God, full of love for the people around him, but that didn't stop him from preaching something that was clearly untrue.

So how do we know truth? The truth we can rely on is the truth of God. That is the truth we find in God's Word. Truth that is consistent with the character of God as shown to us throughout the whole of the Bible.

Sometimes preachers will give you a verse here and a verse there, pull them out of context and then call that truth. But as we've discussed in the introduction, all of Scripture is God-breathed, and that means when we listen to teaching from the Bible, we must make sure it matches up with what God has taught us in the *whole* of the Bible, not just what one or two verses sound like they might mean on their own.

So if you hear a donkey preaching, make sure what they say matches with what you read in the Bible. If you hear your pastor teaching, make sure what they say matches with what you read in the Bible. If your favourite person is telling you spiritual things, check what they say against the Bible, because your affection for them doesn't make the things they say true.

When you hear a great preacher preaching, only follow them as far as they follow Christ. The message doesn't validate the messenger. When some Christian you admire lets you down don't lose heart, the God they spoke of is no less God and no less good now you know the truth of who they are. And if you hear a donkey preaching a great sermon, don't for that reason follow them and live your life like them. At the end of the day, they're a donkey.

Who Can You Trust?

The power of this story is that it causes us to ask, "Then who can we trust?" If the wise people say dumb things, and people who act like donkeys can tell profound truths, are there any reliable people out there? Of course there are. While people will let us down, God does not leave his message and messengers alone and hope that somehow the job will get done. God cares about this world and he wants people to know his love. Just as he was in charge of both Balaam's words and the donkey's voice, he makes sure that, despite the people tasked to share his message, the good news of what he has done for us in Jesus will be made known. There are many people who faithfully share the message of the Bible, and faithfully seek to follow Jesus day by day. Listen to those who are teaching you and watch how they live. As far as they are faithful to God's Word and live like Jesus, you would do well to heed their teaching and follow their example.

Ultimately the unreliability of God's people drives us to seek the God person. Jesus is known as the Word of God (see John 1:14). Only he is wholly reliable in everything he said, and everything he did. When other people let you down, let that drive you to Jesus, who will never let you down and whose words are always trustworthy.

"If two men are fighting and the wife of one of them comes to rescue her husband from his assailant, and she reaches out and seizes him by his private parts, you shall cut off her hand."
– Deuteronomy 25:11-12

4

The Problem of Ball Grabbing

Deuteronomy 25:11-12

A Vital Law

For our next foray into the exciting world of biblical weirdness we're going to look at one of the most important laws in the Bible, found in Deuteronomy 25:11-12:

> If two men are fighting and the wife of one of them comes to rescue her husband from his assailant, and she reaches out and seizes him by his private parts, you shall cut off her hand. Show her no pity.

The question is, what is a law like this doing in the Bible? While I'm sure it's entirely wrong, I like to think that the Trinity were sitting in heaven thinking of laws that God's people might need, and the Father said, "What happens if there are two men fighting, and then one of their wives jumps in and grabs the other man by the testicles? That could be a significant problem."

Then the Holy Spirit might have replied, "Seriously? How often do you think that would happen?"

At which Jesus may have piped up, "As the only one in this Godhead who is actually going to become a man, I feel it's best we make a law about this, just in case!"

But, like I said, I don't think that is how God, in his divine wisdom, wrote laws. So maybe there is another explanation.

Perhaps there was an epidemic of ball grabbing amongst the Israelites. Laws often come about in response to a certain problem. Maybe there were so many squashed grapes in Israel that God snapped and said, "That's it, I've had enough! I'm making a law!"

This is a fascinating question that we may only ever know the answer to when we make it to glory.

Is this Sexism?

There is a problem though. While those of us who are men generally might avoid spending too much time questioning what might seem like a very sensible law (we read it, say

"Amen" and then move on), there might be a few women who think this law is nuts (see what I did there?). They might be wondering why women are getting singled out here. What if a man went for another man's jingle bells? Why isn't there a law about that? Why isn't there a law for if two women are fighting and a husband steps in and punches the other woman in the boob? Shouldn't he also lose his hand?

These are important questions, but you only need to go back a few verses to see that this law doesn't occur in sexist isolation, and it's not about protecting noble fighting men from sneaky junk-grabbing women. When you look back you can see the context of this crazy commandment. Read Deuteronomy 25:5-10 for a clue: it suggests that this law is about protecting future families.

In Bible times having kids was pretty important. Kids were a gift from God and your retirement scheme. There was no superannuation or government pension. When you got old you needed your kids to look after you. In addition to this, kids - sons especially – were the means by which your family name lived on. The ancient Israelites did not have as developed a concept of the afterlife as we have in New Testament Christianity, so for them to live on was primarily seen as occurring through their family legacy. To deprive a person of the ability to have kids, especially sons, was to deprive them of their future both before and after death.

The Unsandaled One

"But what about the sexism?" you might say. Look back at Deuteronomy 25:5-6 and you will see a law that says that if a woman is married to a man and he dies without giving her a son, his brother should marry her and give her a son. The widow should marry her brother-in-law. The son she bears will then take on the woman's dead husband's name. That way she will not be a desolate widow. She will have a husband and a child to look after her when times get tough, and a son to continue the family name and maintain the family inheritance.

You may have noticed a problem. Not all brothers were going to be into this. The brother may have been keen on trying to get his hands on the inheritance himself, and he wouldn't want to create some punk kid who would be taking his brother's property from him. Or perhaps he just wasn't that into his sister-in-law. Whatever the reason the brother might have, there is a law saying that if he refused to marry his sister-in-law, the widow could go to the elders, tell them what he was doing, and the elders would have a chat to him. If he still refused, then his brother's widow was legally allowed to "take off one of his sandals, spit in his face and say, 'This is what is done to the man who will not build up his brother's family line.' That man's line shall be known in Israel as The Family of the Unsandaled" (Deuteronomy 25:9-10).

Now that seems strange enough as it is. Who cares if he has no sandals? Sandals are ugly anyway. Sandals are what your weird uncle wore before he discovered Crocs. I suspect there would be many single men who would much prefer to get spat in the face and be called Jeremy Unsandaled than have to marry their sister-in-law. However, the ancient Israelites lived in a shame- and honour-based culture. To be known as The Unsandaled Family would be a great humiliation. Everyone would know that you were the guy who neglected his familial duties. Plus, all your kids and grandkids would be known by your duty avoidance too. It would be like meeting someone called Frank Child Support-Avoider, only it turned out it wasn't Frank who didn't pay child support, because Frank is five years old and still thinks babies are born out of belly buttons. It was Frank's grandfather, Dropkick Jack, who actually didn't pay his dues, but poor old Frank gets stuck with the name and is always getting teased on the monkey bars because of his deadbeat grandpa. You really wouldn't put your family through that at all. Grandpa Jack would probably just pay the child support.

And what about all this unsandaled business, you ask? In our culture if you flip someone the bird it's pretty rude. In those days feet and shoes were closely linked to signs and rituals of honour and dishonour. If you wanted to insult people and show disrespect to them you could use your feet to great effect. In Psalm 41:9 David writes, "Even my close friend, someone I trusted, one who shared my bread, has turned against me." Where it says "has turned against me" he literally wrote "has lifted his heel against me". If you wanted to show someone how much you hated them, you just flipped them the heel. Even today in Arab cultures showing the bottom of your feet to someone is the height of rudeness. And to throw a shoe at someone is a great insult. An Iraqi journalist did just that to former US President George W. Bush in 2008. Westerners thought it was funny, people in the Middle East knew exactly what was going on. Likewise in the Bible to not have shoes was a sign of dishonour. When the prodigal son came home his dad got him a pair of shoes (see Luke 15:22); it was a sign of his return to honour. So according to this law the dropkick brother who won't marry his sister-in-law loses a shoe, a sign of dishonour. Get it?

The important thing to note here is that God really wants widows looked after, and it's important to him to have brothers-in-law do their duty. Then right after that law we have the law about how wives should get their hands off other men's business. So why are these laws together? It seems they are thematically linked. As the brother-in-law can stop the widow from having kids, the overprotective wife can stop her husband's enemy from having kids. She grabs a bit too hard, and there goes the family. In both these instances God is saying, "Guys, don't stop others from having kids! That's not your right, that's not your responsibility." Family is important to God. Kids are a blessing from God (see Psalm 127:3-5). If we want to learn something from this law it's that God honours family, and if God honours family then we need to honour family too.

Honour Family

How do we honour family? Let's figure that out. For married people and people with kids, this means we need to prioritise our family before anything else but God. We need to love our families. Families are not just something else to be attained along with other life goals – a good career, owning a home, running a marathon, having a great collection of socks, etc. If you have a family they become the priority. You care for them and honour them. If God sees the importance of protecting the ability to create a family, you should see it as of the utmost importance to care for and protect your family.

I suspect many of you reading this don't have a spouse and kids. But while you're still living at home with your parents, and brothers and sisters, you can honour them. As a son or daughter, instead of just waiting till you can be totally independent and escape the clutches of your annoying parentals, you can seek to be a blessing to them. God obviously thinks you're a blessing to them, so you could even live like it! You could seek to serve them, spend time with them, care about their lives in the way they care about yours. When you get older and move out of the house, come back and visit them. When they get older you can make sure you care for them.

Not everyone is going to have good relationships with their parents. Some parents treat their kids horrendously. So maybe you can ask the question, "How can I be a blessing to my parents?" It might be as simple as sending them a text, or refusing to take the bait when you want to blow up at them. Maybe it's sending them a card for their birthday, or praying for them and letting them know that you are doing it. If this feels too difficult, or even impossible, ask God to help you. If he honours family, he'll help you do it too.

Whatever your family situation may be, you can start honouring your family by thanking God for them. Be thankful for your mum and your dad. If you have only a mum, only a dad, or some other parental combination, be thankful. If you have no parents, but you have people who have looked after you, be thankful for them. If you have siblings you can thank God for them too.

What's amazing is that while we have our earthly families, and they don't always work as well as we might like, God loves family so much that, when we trust in Jesus, he gives us a new spiritual family. Because of what Jesus has done for us on the cross we can become God's adopted children (see Galatians 4:4-7). God becomes our loving father, and Jesus becomes our brother. Every other Christian becomes our brother or sister. Psalm 68:5-6 tells us that God is a father to the fatherless, who sets the lonely in families. Psalm 27:10 says, "Though my father and mother forsake me, the LORD will receive me."

You may be too young to have kids now, perhaps you never will. That's okay. You can love and serve God differently, but just as well. In fact, some, like the Apostle Paul, would even say that you can serve God better when you are not focused on caring for a partner and children (see 1 Corinthians 7:32-35). And before you have kids, one more way to honour family is to make sure that family comes at the right time. One of the reasons why Christians say it's important to wait till you're married to have sex is the very practical reality that—spoiler alert—sex makes babies. Having kids outside of marriage can be difficult for the parents and the kids, especially if one of the parents doesn't stick around. Saving sex for marriage honours family by waiting until you can care for a family before you do the business of creating a family, if you know what I mean.

Protect the Jewels

Another way that we can honour family is to make sure we don't get in the way of other people being able to have kids. Don't hurt a man's balls. Stay away from his private parts. Whether you're male or female, leave guy bits alone. Sometimes people think it's funny to try and whack guys in the business, but it's not. Sometimes women like to punish a man by hitting him in the goolies, but they shouldn't. You could damage them, preventing him from having kids in the future because you've decided to hurt him now.

There is one exception to this rule. The only time I feel like it's acceptable to punch the plums is if a man is attacking you. When I was in high school we were visited by an ex-policeman who was teaching young people about sexual assault. For the guys he spent an hour telling us what rape was and what happens to rapists in prison. For the girls he taught them what to do if a man tried to attack them. Eyes, nose, throat, groin, foot. Just hurt them in as many places as possible, as quickly as possible. If a man is attacking you, I think that's a perfect time to knee him in the genitals. If he plans on using them to attack you, you're well within your rights to defend yourself against them.

However, in general, to guys and girls, men and women, protect the future family of a man and his partner – leave the block and tackle alone.

Should We Cut Off the Hand?

Imagine this: a man runs up to their pastor. "Pastor, Pastor!" they shout. "I was just out brawling with Dropkick Jack and his wife came out of nowhere and grabbed my man bits! They are now sore, swollen, and it hurts to sit down! Please grab your axe so we can find this woman and chop off her hand!"

How do you think the pastor should respond? Should he go get the axe and relieve this woman of her offending hand? Obviously the answer is "No". Or is it obvious? If we believe the Bible, shouldn't we be obeying all of it? Why don't we cut off hands, or spit in the face of ceremonially unsandaled men? Why can we eat pork when the Bible says not to (see Deuteronomy 14:8)? Why aren't we executing disobedient children like it says to in Leviticus 20:9?

There are perhaps two things worth noting. The first is that these are laws for an ancient theocracy[1] which none of us live in, so they are not binding for us now. The second is that Jesus has fulfilled the law and called us all to its heart, so we now have a different way we are called to live.

---

1 A theocracy is "a form of government in which God or a deity is recognized as the supreme civil ruler." Thanks, Dictionary.com.

First the theocracy. If you think about when these laws were given it might help you to see why we don't obey them now. This law in Deuteronomy 25 is part of a long speech given by Moses to God's people before they entered the Promised Land. There they would establish themselves as a nation with a land and with laws. Moses was saying, "When you arrive in the land, these are the laws you are to have."

Considering that probably most people reading this book are not in Israel (unless for some reason this book becomes crazy popular in Israel), and nobody reading this book is living in Israel thousands of years ago (unless this book becomes crazy popular with time travellers), we do not need to apply the laws given in the Old Testament in the same way they were intended for the original hearers.

When I was in primary school I had to wear my tie when travelling to and from school. I didn't like this rule and thought it was dumb. I'm sure it had some good reason behind it, but I just hated wearing my tie. Now that I'm no longer in primary school, I can wear a tie when I travel, or I can choose not to. Unless you went to my primary school, you never were under that rule, so it doesn't and never has applied to you. In a similar way, now that you and I are in a different time and place the Old Testament law doesn't apply to us.

But while I don't still go to school so am no longer under the authority of my school, God does still exist and he is still in charge of our lives. God has chosen to operate in the world differently after Jesus than how he did before Jesus came. So we need to work out, how does God want us to live now? What do we need to do to obey now? That's where the second part of our answer comes in.

When Jesus came, he changed how we apply God's law. In the Sermon on the Mount (see Matthew 5-7) we see Jesus telling us what the law says, then showing us what's at the heart of the law so that we might obey God's heart, rather than just the letter of the law.

In Matthew 5:38 Jesus says, "You have heard that it was said, 'Eye for eye, and tooth for tooth.'" He is quoting from Exodus 21:24 and Deuteronomy 19:21. But Jesus doesn't leave it there, he shows us what God's heart behind that law was. He says this:

> But I tell you, do not resist an evil person. If anyone slaps you on the right cheek, turn to them the other cheek also. And if anyone wants to sue you and take your shirt, hand over your coat as well. If anyone forces you to go one mile, go with them two miles. Give to the one who asks you, and do not turn away from the one who wants to borrow from you. (Matthew 5:39-42)

While God gave the original law to limit the amount of retaliation people might seek when they had been wronged, this is not God's ultimate goal for humanity. God's goal is that we would actually *love* other people. God wants us to be people who never seek to hurt others, or exact our own revenge, but repay evil with love and leave the rest to God (see Romans 12:17-21). God's people are to change his world with love.

For the followers of Jesus the centre of God's law is that we would love God and love others (see Luke 10:25-28). This is the way that we are called to live that sums up all the laws of the Old Testament. If you want to see the laws that apply to us now, the new way of doing things for people who no longer live in ancient Israel, you need only look at the New Testament. Here we see what it means to love God and love others. Many of the moral laws from the Old Testament are repeated here, many others are distilled to their pure essence. All of them show us God's heart, and how he wants us to live now.

This is all very nice, but also incredibly hard. None of us loves anyone perfectly. And that's the last part of the answer to the question of whether we should still be cutting people's hands off. In the Old Testament, God gave laws about how to deal with things when people broke his law. It was through a system of sacrifices that Israel's sin was dealt with, but all these sacrifices were only pointing to what Jesus was going do at the cross when his death paid the penalty for the sins of humanity. That is why Jesus could say he did not come to abolish the law but to fulfill it (see Matthew 5:17), and Paul could say that Jesus "is the culmination of the law so that there may be righteousness for everyone who believes" (Romans 10:4).

We don't need to cut off any grabby hands, because Jesus fulfilled that law and gave us a new way to live. But out of neighbourly love it's best you don't grab your male neighbour's beanbag and avoid busting his nuts. It's not the godly way.

To sum up, honour family, love Jesus, and don't hurt the nuts.

"Ehud reached with his left hand, drew the sword from his right thigh and plunged it into the king's belly. Even the handle sank in after the blade, and his bowels discharged." – Judges 3:21-22

5

The Fat, the Poo, and the Left-handed Man

Judges 3:12-30

Introducing Ehud

This story is about a guy called Ehud. I love Ehud. What a man! Why people rarely talk about him in church I don't know. He seems to be relegated to kids' talks and youth groups. Probably because he's too awesome so adults find him intimidating.

Ehud is the second judge in the book of Judges. Judges is an intriguing book. It's about God's people in the Promised Land. They were trying to get themselves established but they were not doing a very good job of it. Throughout the book they're on this perpetual cycle of stuff-ups, starting with their awkward decision to worship other gods. They found the gods of the surrounding nations rather attractive so they started worshipping them. This caused them to come under God's curse and other nations moved in to rule over and oppress them. As you would expect, they didn't like this, so they cried out to God asking to be set free. God heard their cries and, ever merciful, he raised up a series of individuals to save his people. These folk were the judges. Each judge in turn fought against Israel's enemies, won, and set them free. Israel responded by worshipping God for a while but eventually, the ruling judge died and Israel went back to their old habits of worshipping other gods. They then came under God's curse and it all started again. That's the Judges cycle. Ehud rocks up near the beginning of the book and he's definitely my favourite character in Judges. Certainly much better than Samson (see Judges 13-16) or the dude who murdered his daughter (see Judges 11). Why do I love him? Let me show you.

Ehud the Left-handed Hero

It all starts when Israel "did evil" (drugs, arms dealing, microwaving kittens, the usual bad guy stuff[1]) and came under the rule of a group of people called the Moabites. The Moabite king was a guy called Eglon. We don't know much about Eglon except that he was fat (see Judges 3:17). He was probably fat because he ruled over other nations, stole their food, produce,

---

1 Actually it's probably more like worshipping other gods. But let's not allow facts to get in the way of a good story.

and treasure, and gorged himself on the spoils. So Israel, being "fatists", and not enthusiastic about being under the foreign rule of a man who stole their potatoes and waffles, cried out to God. God heard and raised up your friend and mine, Ehud the Judge.

Now Ehud was a pretty cool guy. For one, we're told that he was a left-handed man which seems to be implying that he was tricky. That's right, people have been wary of those shifty lefties since Old Testament days. Which is exactly what made Ehud so perfect for the role he was about to play. However, the mention of Ehud's left-handedness might not actually be about his trickiness - what it actually says in the original Hebrew is that he was restricted in his right. This could mean that he had a deformed right hand. Maybe it got crushed under a millstone, burnt in a fire, or bitten off by a shark. If something had happened to his hand we don't exactly know what it is, but for some reason he can't use it.

The other excellent thing about Ehud is that it tells us in Judges 3:16 that he made his own double-edged sword. That's pretty bad-ass. He's restricted in his right hand, just like Luke Skywalker, and he makes his own weapons, à la John Rambo. This guy is a mash-up of two of the coolest characters in filmic history. I'm surprised there isn't a movie about him from the 80s and at least one remake!

But I digress. As we continue the story we read that our hero and some of his mates were on their way to meet Eglon. Eglon, as noted before, was very fat. This was a guy who spent too little time on the rowing machine and too much time on the gravy. But being fat doesn't stop you from ruling another country, it just stops you from looking good in Lycra while doing it. So Ehud and his friends were off to pay tribute to Eglon on behalf of Israel. When one country pays tribute to another it's a symbol of their inferiority. One country might pay money, or grain, or something else to say, "You are more powerful than us, we live in submission to you."

It's like in *The Hunger Games* when they randomly select two kids from every district to fight to the death, and Katniss Everdeen jumps up and says, "I volunteer as tribute." The tributes are a sign of each district's submission to the Capitol. And that's also what's going on here with Ehud and the Israelites. Their Katniss Everdeen may not be fighting anyone to the death, but Israel, through their gifts, were demonstrating to Moab that they were their submissive subjects.

Once the tribute had been paid, Ehud said to his friends that he had to return to see the king. When he arrived, Ehud said to the king, "Your majesty, I have a secret message for you" (v. 19). At least that's what our English translations say, but what the original Hebrew literally says is, "Your majesty, I have a secret thing for you." The thing could be anything, a word, an object, a donut – anything. The king interpreted this to be a secret message and got very excited because he just loved secrets, so he sent everybody away. This was a stupid, stupid thing to do. If you learn nothing else from this passage, learn this: if you ever happen to become a ruler over a subjected people, never let yourself be alone with them. Imagine you become the ruler over some poor, weaker nation, like say, New Zealand. If a Kiwi comes to you and says, "I have a secret for you" do not send all your bodyguards away. They will kill you, those sneaky, left-handed Kiwis,[2] and that's exactly what happens here.

Eglon and Ehud were all alone. When Ehud said, "I have a message from God for you" (v. 20), the king responded, "Ooh, ooh, what is it? I'm so excited!" and he raised his very large frame from the throne, presenting a full belly to Ehud. Ehud reached with his left hand to his right side (a sneaky move that only a left-handed warrior could do), grabbed his double-edged dagger (probably in slow motion), and whispered in the king's ear, "Here's God's message" as he plunged his blade into the king's ample belly. Eglon was so fat that his rolls closed in over the handle. And then comes one of the greatest parts in the entire Bible, Judges 3:22. What the old NIV translation of the Bible used to say was this:

> Even the handle sank in after the blade, which came out his back. Ehud did not pull the sword out, and the fat closed in over it. (NIV 1984)

This in itself was pretty great. Sword out the back? Awesome! But now, the NIV has been updated to better reflect the original intent of the verse and it's even awesomer. It says this:

---

2 I actually have nothing against Kiwis. A bunch of my relatives are Kiwi and as far as I know they're all very honest, even the left-handed ones.

> Even the handle sank in after the blade, and his bowels
> discharged. Ehud did not pull the sword out, and the fat
> closed in over it.

The king got stabbed so hard that he pooped himself! Let me
tell you what a serious, biblical scholar said: "At this climactic
moment, without the dagger being removed, Eglon's anal
sphincter explodes!"[3] That is biblical scholarship at its finest,
if you ask me! Michael Bay has exploding buildings, planes,
and robots. The Bible has an exploding sphincter! Obviously
the Bible *is* the greatest book in the history of the world. It tells
us of God's glorious plan for salvation and has faeces exploding
out of a stabbed, evil, fat man! Doesn't this show us that God
speaks to all people through his Word, even those of us who are
hilariously immature?

Once the deed was done, Ehud took his chance to escape. He
ran over to the doors, locked them from the inside and escaped
through the porch. Meanwhile the king's stewards found the
locked door and, sniffing the air, sensed the king's personal
aroma and left the king alone.

> Steward 1: Can you smell that? It smells like
> the dead love child of Jabba the Hutt and a
> tuna fish - I'd know that smell anywhere. The
> king must be relieving himself!
>
> *Time passes*

---

3 K. Lawson Younger, *The NIV Application Commentary: Judges/
Ruth*, Grand Rapids: Zondervan, 2011, p. 118.

Steward 2: This is getting embarrassing now. Maybe he's fallen asleep.

S1: Maybe the smell gave him a concussion.

S2: Maybe he's run out of toilet paper, I suspect something that pungent requires a significant clean-up operation.

More time passes

S1: We really should go in and have a look.

S2: Wowsers! Who died in here? Oh, someone actually did.

S1: Good one, Neville.

The stewards waited so long that Ehud had the perfect opportunity to get away. The whole time that they were standing around embarrassed, thinking that the king was relieving himself, Ehud was making his escape. It was the trusty poo diversion, oldest trick in the book, still used by the SAS and Delta Force to this day.

When Ehud arrived back with his party he grabbed a horn and blew it, rounding up all his fellow countrymen, telling them, "Follow me, for the LORD has given Moab, your enemy, into your hands" (v. 28). Everyone fought the Moabites, the Israelites won, not a single Moabite escaped, Israel was liberated and they lived in freedom for eighty years.

The End.

The Picture of Jesus

Can you see why this is such a great story? Would you be surprised if I told you that Ehud is a picture of Jesus?

Yup, let me show you.

Firstly, at the beginning we see how Israel, because of their evil, had come under subjugation to an evil power. We are people who have also come under subjugation because of our sin. Not to a foreign power, but to the rule of Satan, sin, and death.

Then God's people cried out to him for salvation. Not out of repentance, just out of distress at being under the rule of another nation. So God sent Ehud to deliver them. Likewise, the Bible tells us that while we were still sinners Christ died for us (see Romans 5:8). God saw our plight and he didn't even wait for us to cry out to him before he sent Jesus to die for us so that we might be forgiven and set free.

Yet while Ehud, the sneaky left-hander, defeated the king by stabbing him in the guts, Jesus, in the most "left-handed" action in history, defeated Satan, sin, and death, by allowing himself, the King of kings, to be killed.

And now, just as Ehud called his people to follow him to freedom, Jesus is risen from death and calls us to follow him.

Now I'm not saying that Ehud and Jesus are the same - Jesus didn't do any stabbing - but God loves to save his people. We see this again and again throughout the Bible. We see it through Ehud, and we see it best displayed in Jesus. God is a God who saves his people in unexpected ways. He saved his people unexpectedly through a left-handed man who stabbed a fat king, and he saves his people through a non-violent, homeless teacher, who is killed on a cross. That is unexpected.

God Saves Despite Us

Whenever the Bible teaches us about the character of God, there is something for us to learn about how we need to relate to God in light of who he is. This passage is no different.

The first thing we notice is that God will save, even when the heart is wrong.

In this story Israel recognised they had a problem, but made no attempt to deal with its root cause. They just cried out to God to save them and he did. They didn't repent, they didn't change their ways, and they were back in the same situation again in the very next chapter of Judges. Despite this, God saved them. He didn't wait for them to get themselves right with him before he saved them, he heard their cry and he acted. This is because when God saves it's not about the character of those who are being saved, it is all about the glory of the one who is *doing* the saving.

So often we feel that before we can cry out to God for help we have to make sure we're right with him. We want to make sure we have the right attitude, that we aren't sinning, that we're praying and reading the Bible. We feel like we can't ask for forgiveness until we know we've dealt with our sin. Only once we think we have ourselves sorted out do we feel we can call out to God. It's as though we must do everything within our power to save ourselves before bothering God. But that's absurd! What's the point of being saved by God if you've already saved yourself? Jesus said, "It's not the healthy who need a doctor, but the sick" (Luke 5:31).

Back in my single days, like many single people do, I would often contemplate getting into relationships. I would think myself into all sorts of contortions. I would think, "If I ask a girl on a date, what if on the date I realise I don't like her, and then I have to stop going on dates with her? That'd be awkward. Or what if we're going on dates and then we start dating but I don't really know if I want to date her? Do I need to figure out if I love her before we start dating? Or what if we're in a relationship for like two years and then we're planning to get married, but I realise I don't want to marry her and then I break her heart? So really before I go on a date to begin with I should figure out if I want to marry her." I would try and get everything sorted all at the beginning. But you can't solve every potential problem that might arise before you even go on your first date, that's why you go on dates, to get to know each other, to figure things out, to see if you're compatible. If you try and get everything sorted before your first date you'll never go on a date, you'll be forever alone.

To some degree we treat God like that. We say, "I'm not going to come to God until my heart is in the right place." But we're not going to date God. We need to think of him less like a person to date and more like a lifesaver.

If you're in the ocean and you're drowning you're not going to stop and think to yourself, "Before I cry out for help, I had better get myself in order. First I had better work out my motivations. Do I want to be saved so I can not drown, or do I want to be saved so I can know this lifesaver? And am I really sorry for getting caught in the rip? Will I do it again? Maybe I should learn to swim a bit better, and get myself to safety before I call out for the lifesaver. Then the lifesaver won't be disappointed when they come out to me and discover my inability to swim at this point in time. I'd hate to disappoint the lifesaver." If you're drowning, you cry out for help, you can worry about the rest later.

That's how we must relate to God. Don't wait to get yourself right with God before you cry out to him. Don't wait to make sure you're praying, reading your Bible, not sinning, that you really are sorry, and you really do love God. Who cares? If you're in trouble, call out to him, he'll hear you. Don't wait till your heart is right before you cry out to him, or you'll never do it. In fact, the first step in getting your heart right *is* to cry out to him. If you spend all your time trying to get your heart in order before you call out to him, you'll miss the first and most important step of faith and that's to realise that you cannot save yourself, you need God! You can't sort out your heart without him. So stop trying to get right for him, and just call out.

If you're not a follower of Jesus you need to call out to God to save you; from your own sin, from the punishment that you deserve, and from your captivity to death. Don't wait till you've got your life in order; till you've stopped swearing, or drinking, or you're out of that unhealthy relationship. God wants to save you as you are. He'll save you because he is good, not because you're well behaved. Cry out to him.

If you're a Christian, don't ever think that you can't cry out to God. No matter what your sin is like, no matter how well or badly you're doing in your relationships with him or others. No matter how close or far away from him you feel, when you need him, cry out to him. Don't wait to get your heart right. God didn't wait till Israel was right with him before he saved them. God didn't wait for you to get right before he sent Jesus, he didn't even wait for you to exist. God wants to hear from you however your heart is. And he wants to answer your cries, because when he saves it's not about how bad you are but about how great he is. Cry out to him.

God's Unlikely Means

The second thing we can see from this story is that God will save even when the means are unlikely. He doesn't use the people you'd expect in the way you'd expect.

When you look at Ehud you can see that he isn't really some great poster boy for righteousness. He's awesome, but he's not exactly honest. And he doesn't get the king in a stand up fight. He's sneaky and stabs the king when the king thinks he's about to get a present or a cheeseburger or something. With Ehud, we don't even know why he did what he did. There's no indication that he did what he did out of obedience to God. God never speaks to him. He just took matters into his own hands (or at least his own left hand) and headed off to stab the king. That's not exactly exemplary behaviour. It's a pretty bad idea to just decide for yourself to go knife the leader of a nation. Still, God used Ehud to save his people. God will save even when the means seem unlikely.

If God could use Ehud then that means that God can use you and me also. You might have issues, but chances are you're not a sneaky, poo-stabbing, rogue assassin.

God has a long and glorious history of using unlikely people for his glory. In this story he was using both Ehud and Eglon for his purposes. He uses flawed kings, leaders, and prophets in the Old Testament. He spread his gospel through a bunch of dull cowards in the New Testament. And he saved the world through a man who was poor, homeless, and executed. God uses unlikely people in unlikely ways, so he can and will use you. Character, position, talent, and skills are not prerequisites for usefulness in God's kingdom. Expect God to use you, because he can and he will.

That doesn't mean just be as sinful as you want and God will still use you. After all, God used Eglon and we saw how that ended up. It just means don't write yourself or anyone else off as a vessel for God to use. He will always be working to save no matter how unlikely the tools. So stop sitting around waiting till you're good enough for God to use, and start getting the job done. Start loving the people around you, get involved in that ministry at church, pray for your friends, tell that person you met about Jesus. God can and will even use unlikely you, so get going.

God Saves When Things Seem Hopeless

Finally, don't give up hope because God will save, even when the situation seems hopeless.

Israel had no idea that God was saving them until the biggest job was already done. Ehud took it upon himself to defeat Eglon, and it was this defeat that led to Ehud being able to lead the people of Israel to victory. The people weren't all working together to kick out the Moabites. There was no grassroots campaign, there were no stirrings of revolution, there was nothing – and then suddenly Eglon was dead and Ehud was leading them to victory. God heard their cries and worked even when nothing seemed to be happening.

You may look at your own life, and look at all the things that seem hopeless. You may look at your friends who don't know Jesus, the relationships that look like they'll never be reconciled, the sin you don't think you can beat, the sickness that looks like it'll never be healed, and think that God is never going to do anything, but you don't know what God is doing behind the scenes. Things may seem hopeless, but God is always working.

Nobody knew that God was working to save Israel until he'd done it. Nobody understood how God was going to save the world through Jesus until he'd done it. And if God has already saved us through Jesus, if he's already beaten Satan, sin, and death, then why would he not keep working? God will work, even when the situation seems hopeless, so don't give up hope. He may not work in all the ways you're expecting and hoping that he'll work, but he will work.

This story of Ehud and the fat king, it's exciting and it's funny. More than that it's a fantastic illustration of the saving character of God, who works to save his people when they cry out, even when their hearts are in the wrong place; who works to save, even through the most unlikely of people; who saves even when the situation seems most hopeless. God is a God who saves. It's in his character, that's why he would save even you and even me.

6

David and the Foreskins

1 Samuel 18:12-30

I spent a lot of my teenage years trying to figure out how to woo various women. Actually, mostly it was just plans to woo one woman. She was in my year at school, and I liked her for four years straight. I dreamed up many schemes for convincing her of my love, often involving us accidentally getting stuck in an elevator together where she would have no choice but to chat to me for hours on end. During this time she would discover how wonderful I was and we'd make out until we were rescued, exiting the elevator having both discovered true love. As it was, I never managed to engineer us being in a lift alone together, let alone organise it to break down for hours on the off-chance that we might kiss a lot and subsequently begin a lifelong romance.

My secret plans may seem a little crazy but they are nothing compared to the way that David won the hand of his bride. I wanted to use a lift, he used a bunch of foreskins,[1] and none of them were his. This is one strange story.

David's Romcom

Our story begins when David (the very same David who killed Goliath, became a king, wrote some psalms, stole someone's wife and murdered her husband) was rising up the ranks of King Saul's army before he himself would become king. David was having great success in defeating the Philistines, the enemies of Israel. Women thought David was just the very best and would sing songs about him, much like women have been known to sing songs about me.[2] They would sing, "Saul has slain his thousands, and David his tens of thousands" (1 Samuel 18:7).

Saul, who was extremely jealous of all David's admirers, decided the best thing to do would be to have David killed. By this point Saul had tried a few different tactics to dispose of David: he had tried throwing spears at David, but that never worked; he had

---

1 Don't know what a foreskin is? Look it up in the dictionary, *not* on Google Images.

2 This is a lie. No one but me has sung songs about me.

sent David into battle, hoping he would die at the hands of his enemies, but David kept coming back alive. I guess they were rather incompetent enemies. The only thing left was marriage. I know, marriage is generally not life threatening, but Saul had a cunning plan.

Saul suggested that David marry his daughter and then, because David was now part of the family, he would have to fight bravely for Saul and hopefully then he would get killed.[3] Saul was working hard to fulfill his role as the scary father-in-law. At first Saul offered his eldest daughter, Merab, however, when David opened negotiations by suggesting that he wasn't worthy to become Saul's son-in-law (translation: "Yes please! I'd love to marry your daughter, I'm just too polite to say so"), Saul withdrew the offer and married her off to someone else (vv. 18-19).

But then, changing his mind, Saul once again decided it was a good idea to have David marry his daughter, so he offered Michal. As it turned out, Michal was in love with David. She'd seen him walking around the place with his ruddy good looks, his massive, warrior muscles, and his beautiful singing voice, and she knew he was the one for her. Saul thought this was a much better match, so he offered David a second chance to become his son-in-law. Saul sent servants to say, "Look, the king likes you, and his attendants all love you; now become

---

3 In 2 Samuel 11 David uses a similar ploy to deal with the husband of his lover Bathsheba. This time it works and Bathsheba's husband is killed. Poor form, Davo!

his son-in-law" (v. 22). When Michal heard her father wanted her to marry David she probably felt like all her dreams had come true. Perhaps her feelings were similar to what I would have felt had I found myself in that long imagined elevator when suddenly it got stuck halfway between floors 7 and 8 and the emergency operator told my crush and me that the lift technicians were about seven hours away, so we should hug to conserve body heat (it was a legitimate fantasy when I was fourteen). That is to say, Michal would have felt ecstatic.

David began negotiations again with another humble response: "Do you think it is a small matter to become the king's son-in-law? I'm only a poor man and little known" (translation: "Yes please! But I can't afford the bride-price for your daughter") (v. 23).

This was all part of Saul's plan. He worked out an arrangement so that David wouldn't have to sell his harp to win his bride. All he had to do was bring Saul one hundred Philistine foreskins. Saul was thinking that David would go out to collect the foreskins and get killed in the process, because collecting foreskins isn't as easy as, say, collecting one hundred Burger Rings. David wasn't going to be able to walk up to the Philistine men and say, "Hey! I wonder if you can do me a favour? I really like this girl, and I want to marry her and impress her dad. I'm wondering if you'll do me a favour and just let me cut off a small bit of your penis?" While I assume the Philistines loved a love story as much as the next guy, their response would have been, "No! Get lost, you pervert! I'm keeping all my willy for me!"

So David was going to have to kill the men before they parted with even a small part of their manhood. That was the cunning in Saul's plan. The Philistines were going to fight tooth, nail, and dong to stay fully intact. Saul was hoping David got killed somewhere in that process.

Unfortunately for Saul, David and his men were master foreskin hunters and David came back with 200 of those bad boys! I suspect this process was a little embarrassing for David and his men. They would have rushed in, stabbed the Philistines, then, hoping no one was looking, pulled up their man-skirts, chopped off the end of their members, and then collected them. I wonder though, did David have a small foreskin purse that he took into that particular battle? Did he get his men to do it? Or did they all refuse, saying, "Look, we love you, Chief, but you're going to have to violate the corpses yourself!" Plus David did it 200 times, that's twice the amount necessary! You've got to really want to marry a girl to get into that sort of business. The only small circular object I got for my wife before our wedding was an engagement ring - thankfully that was enough.

David and his men returned to Saul with his haul of skin rings and the Bible says, "They counted out the full number to the king so that David might become the king's son-in-law" (v. 27). Imagine that! On second thought, perhaps don't. That's one weird ceremony: "One foreskin, two foreskins . . . 200 foreskins! Now, marriage!"

Here's something else not to ponder too deeply: What did Saul want with 200 foreskins anyway? Was he going to make a necklace? Maybe some matching earrings? He could start an Etsy store selling his exclusive line of foreskin jewellery.

Still, it all worked out, David got the girl and Saul's plan was foiled yet again.

God is Going to Do What God is Going to Do

That is one heck of a story, full of wholesome adventure and circumcision, what all great epics are made of. But once again we're left asking the question, "What do we learn from this?"

Firstly, it's important to remember that not every story in the Bible, even if it contains a hero of the faith, is necessarily something the Bible wants you to do. If you're trying to convince someone to love you this story isn't condoning killing a bunch of men and cutting off a small part of their genitals. It's just telling you that it happened. If you are trying to woo someone, perhaps consider getting them a nice card, or flowers and chocolates. Alternatively, a strategically engineered elevator emergency could work. Anything but grand scale penile mutilation.

However, there is more to this story than ancient marriage rituals. It's important to remember that David was God's anointed king. Since 1 Samuel 16 God has been planning to put David on the throne of Israel, but it's not until 2 Samuel 2 that David becomes king of anywhere. There is a lot of time in between for things to go wrong and Saul did his very best to thwart God's plans. Saul wanted to hold on to power and he didn't want an upstart like David taking his fame and adulation, let alone his throne. But no matter how much Saul tries to stop David, he can't because no one can stop God from doing what God is going to do. This is an important lesson for us to learn. We can either get on board with God's agenda, or we can fight against it, but one way or another God is going to do what God is going to do.

We see this all through the Bible. In the Exodus, Pharaoh tried to stop God's people from leaving Egypt, but by the hand of God they left anyway. In Jonah we see the prophet trying to avoid sharing the merciful message of God, but a giant storm, a large fish, and one horrid seafood vomit later, Jonah finds himself conforming to the will of God. In the Gospels we see the religious authorities attempt to end Jesus' life, inadvertently setting in motion the events that would save the world and prove that Jesus is not just an influential man, but also the Lord of the universe. In Acts, those same religious authorities tried to shut down the spread of the gospel, but by their persecution they instead enabled the spread of the gospel! God's going to do what God's going to do. You can't stop God!

We may not be able to figure out exactly what God is doing right now, but we're going to see it very clearly at the end of time. The Bible promises that one day every knee will bow and every tongue will confess that Jesus Christ is Lord (see Philippians 2:10-11). That means that worshipping Jesus as Lord for every person in existence is not a question of if but when. One day

Jesus is going to return to this earth and every person will know then and there that the creator of the world, the one who sustains the universe, the ruler of all time and space, once came to earth as a baby, grew to be a man, died for the sins of the world, and rose again. This God-man deserves all glory and adoration, and he will get all glory and adoration. Those of us who know Jesus worship him now willingly, but in the end *all* will worship him – either by choice or by the sheer force of his glory. The universe exists for the glory of God and we'd best get on board with what God is doing before we are made to get on board with what God is doing.

Saul thought he could resist the will of God, but it didn't work; David was always going to be king no matter how much he fought it. Neither can we resist the will of God. One day all of us will worship him. If you don't know Jesus, now is the time to commit your life to him. He has risen from the dead so that you might know that he is Lord, trust in him, and receive life. Do not make the mistake of thinking you can escape. You can honour him now and receive forgiveness for your sins, and live life with him forever, or you can honour him when he returns and you stand before the judge of the world whom you have spent your life rejecting. The choice is yours.

Waxing and Conforming to the Pattern of Christ

If you are a Christian, the challenge for you is to conform your life to the pattern of Christ. The promise of Romans 8:29 is that everyone who is truly saved is destined to be "conformed to the image of [God's] Son." That is God's will for your life –

to make you like Jesus. The problem for us is that to become like Jesus is a long and painful task. All those things we love more than Jesus, all that sin which affects how we live our life – jealousy, pride, anger, greed, laziness – has to be rooted out and destroyed. Jesus said that if we are in him, bearing fruit, God's going to prune us (see John 15:2) so we can lead even better lives for him. Pruning hurts.

The life of a Christian is difficult. We have to deal with the general pain of life, and we have to experience the pain of God smashing our idols and cutting out our sin. The end result is beautiful, but the road there hurts more than circumcision. God will do what God is going to do. Saul spent most of his life seeking to fight against the will of God and things went very badly for him (see 1 Samuel 31). David, though he made mistakes, submitted himself to God and was a man after God's own heart (see Acts 13:22). The question is, how much of a willing participant will you be? Once you have given your life to Jesus, you are his, he is going to change you whether you like it or not. Best you go willing, willing to seek to conform your life to the pattern of Jesus, willing to join him in seeking out your sin and destroying your idols, because it's going to happen anyway. It's best you are a willing participant in the pruning. It'll hurt less.

I once went on a buck's weekend with a bunch of Christian guys. Christians can't (or at least shouldn't) get drunk or get strippers so we have to find other ways to make our buck's parties fun. As a result we usually just seek ways to cause pain to the buck and anyone else on the buck's weekend. It's dumb and I hate it, but that's the way it goes. Anyway, on this weekend the boys had brought a bunch of waxing strips along – the kind women, and anyone else who likes to be hairless, use to remove their leg hair, arm hair, back hair, and other miscellaneous hair. They stick it on the hairy part then rip it off, tearing out all the hair stuck to the strip at the same time and leaving behind smooth and silky skin.

Periodically throughout the weekend a bunch of guys would run up to another man, wrestle him to the ground, find his hairiest body part that wasn't covered by underwear, whack on the wax strip and rip it off. The victim would struggle, fight, and try to avoid this torture, but he would always lose, both the fight and a large chunk of his hair. Watching this I realised at some point they would come for me. I could try and fight but I had watched bigger men than me, men trained in mixed martial arts, fight and lose. I wasn't going to win this fight. So I decided when the wax strip came I would just accept my smooth and silky fate with dignity and poise.

We were 50km from home and an hour from safety when they came for me. I was standing in line at McDonalds. They approached me with wax strips. All I said was "Okay" and that was it. One on the leg, one on the arm. I am not an un-hairy man (except on my head which is rebelling against the dress code of every other part of my body). They tore the strips off. I stood there and pretended it didn't hurt a bit. Inside I cried, and swore, and thought of exacting violent revenge on each and every person involved. On the outside I looked like Mother Teresa, if she was a thirty-year-old balding man in McDonalds.

"Wow!" one of them said. "You're like Gandhi!" I took that as a compliment and then went off to contemplate the torture our culture expects women to go through to conform to society's standards of beauty.

God is coming for you. He's going to make you like Jesus, and it's not some arbitrary, dumb buck's party ritual. This is the transformation of your soul to become the person God always made you to be. Don't resist the work of the Spirit. In fact run to it. Embrace the transformation. Confess your sin to God. Get your Christian friends to join the fight, tell them what you're working on, how God is changing you. Ask them to help you live for Jesus. Daily ask the Holy Spirit to help you become more like Jesus. God is going to make you into the person he wants you to be. Don't fight it, it'll only hurt more.

The Picture of Jesus

Finally there is one more amazing thing about this passage. In it we see a picture of Jesus. You're probably thinking, "Sure! The story of a man cutting off a bunch of other men's special skin at the behest of a jealous king is a picture of Jesus." I assure you it is. In the story David was sent out to win his bride, and he did it with daring and skill and by humiliating and killing hundreds of men. In the Bible we are told that the church (everyone who loves and trusts Jesus) is the bride of Christ (see Ephesians 5:21-33; Revelation 21:1-3). Jesus loves us so much that he came to win his bride for himself. Though we were in the clutches of Satan, sin and death, Jesus won us for himself, not with 200 foreskins, but through his death on the cross. He did not kill and humiliate others to win his bride, but he allowed himself to be stripped naked, humiliated, and killed at the cross so that we might be clothed in the dignity of his salvation. That is the price that he paid to win his bride. So if you want a reason to trust in Jesus now, to honour him now, to bow your knee to him now, then this is it - his love for you at the cross. It is God's will that you worship and trust in his son Jesus. May we all do it before we are forced to. Christ is the great bridegroom who showed us what true love looks like when he won us, his bride, at the cross – at the cost of his life.

"Then two bears came out of the woods and mauled forty-two of the boys." – 2 Kings 2:24

7

Elisha and the Ultimate Fighting Bears

2 Kings 2:23-25

Imagine you're walking along and you see someone who has made your life difficult. Maybe they have been rude to you, maybe they have teased you in public, maybe they egged your house, or have refused to like any of your photos on Instagram. Whatever they did, they upset you, and you don't feel much love for them. You may have the love that is required because you follow Jesus, but certainly no extra love. Then suddenly, flying out of nowhere, a bird, a big bird (not Big Bird, he can't fly) swoops down out of the sky and does a huge poop right on the top of this person's head. It's beautiful, you feel amazing, it's like all of nature is resonating with the cry of your heart and pooping steaming justice on the heads of your enemies. Actually, imagine if Big Bird could fly! I'm sure his poops would reek of their own special retribution.

In this story I suspect our hero, the prophet Elisha, would have felt a similar feeling of vindication. That is, as long as he wasn't too put off by the sight of gallons of blood, severed limbs and screaming teenagers, which I guess might be a little bit more horrifying than a giant bird poop.

This story takes place just after Elijah, the great prophet of Israel, has been taken up into heaven in a whirlwind[1] so Elisha has been given Elijah's ministry as prophet to the people of Israel. Elijah has passed on his mantle to Elisha and this story in 2 Kings 2 is the third in a series of signs that confirm Elisha as God's true prophet. In the first of the signs Elisha hits the river Jordan with Elijah's cloak and it parts so he can cross on dry land (you know, like Moses). In the second sign he uses salt to turn bad water good, showing that through him God can bring blessing. And then we come to the third sign ...

Dem Bears

Elisha was in Bethel and as he was walking along the road he came across a bunch of youths. They were all standing around

---

1 Here's some trivia for you. Many people think Elijah went up to heaven in a flaming chariot, which is much cooler than a whirlwind, but 2 Kings 2:11 says: "As they were walking along and talking together, suddenly a chariot of fire and horses of fire appeared and separated the two of them, and Elijah went up to heaven in a whirlwind."

in a gang, loitering on the street like youths do. They were dealing drugs, doin' graffiti, and listening to the hip hop. Old ladies all over Bethel were terrified. When the youths saw Elisha they noticed his exceptionally bald head, shining like a beacon of righteousness in the Middle Eastern sun. So they hitched up their bum bags, started to tease him, and got all up in his face. They were yelling hurtful things like, "Get out of here, baldy! ... Get out of here ..." (2 Kings 2:23).

Elisha was not gonna let that stand. He was all, "Oh you don't wanna be doin' that, you don't wanna be disrespectin' me."

And they responded, "Oh yeah, whatcha gonna do about it? Get out of here, baldy, get out!"

So he called down a curse on them in God's name, and suddenly out of the woods came two angry bears who mauled forty-two of the mouthy youths.

I think it's amazing that the bears managed to get forty-two of them. That is an exceptionally high number. Either these bears were super fast, and they could take out forty-two boys in seconds, or these boys were super dumb. Perhaps the bears came out, mauled two of them and the boys thought, "Oh no you don't!" and two more rushed in to fight the bears, they got mauled and so more rushed in. You'd think that at some point, like maybe after thirty-five of their friends lost a limb, they'd realise they were getting slaughtered and they would just run away, but the bears managed to get forty-two of them! Forty-two! That's a lot of mauling.

And when that was done, Elisha "went on to Mount Carmel and from there returned to Samaria" (v. 25) like nothing ever happened. This guy is boss.

What the Heck?

So what's going on here, you ask? Is Elisha just particularly sensitive about his hair loss? I'm losing my hair; does this story mean I get to call down bears on people who tease me? Unfortunately for me, and bald men everywhere, this story doesn't seem to be about justice for the follicly challenged.

This story is a confirmation of Elisha's status as a prophet. Bethel was a centre for the worship of idols and chances are, knowing that Elisha wouldn't like their idol worship, the people of Bethel weren't too impressed with the prophet coming to visit them. The kids who mocked Elisha may very well have heard their parents muttering about how much they didn't like him, and thought they'd see if they could take care of Elisha. Unfortunately for them, Elisha was a powerful man of God and they ended up on the pointy end of some bear claws.

You might be thinking, how can God do this to these children?

Firstly, I can't defend God's actions, but why should I have to? We get very upset when bad things happen to children and that's appropriate. However, God's value system is different to ours, and he is free to operate differently to us. He is God and he doesn't have to behave in a way that we feel is appropriate for his actions to be morally righteous. Who are we to judge

God? However, let me at least point out that the text says the bears mauled the youths, they didn't kill them. Some of you may be perfectly comfortable with kids getting a good mauling to teach them a lesson, just as long as they don't die. I did once hear this passage used in a kids' talk to illustrate why they should be respectful of their elders: "Be kind to your mother or bears will get you."

Secondly, this passage is a fulfilment of Leviticus 26:21-22 which outlines the penalty for those who will not listen to God:

> If you remain hostile toward me and refuse to listen to me, I will multiply your afflictions seven times over, as your sins deserve. I will send wild animals against you, and they will rob you of your children, destroy your cattle and make you so few in number that your roads will be deserted.

When there was as much idol worship happening among God's people as there was in Elisha's time, God was going to act and there would be consequences.

Our Leaders are God's Leaders

Finally, because Elisha was God's prophet, when you mocked him you mocked God. When Elisha spoke, God spoke. So when the youths mocked Elisha, the bears came out not to protect Elisha's bald-headed dignity but to cement God's honour. When you mock God's prophet, it's as if you're mocking God. Elisha was God's mouthpiece, so God was going to stick up for him.

That's important for us to notice because what got the boys in trouble was not their disrespect for those of the shiny-headed persuasion, but their lack of respect for God's leader. While we do not have prophets today like they had in the Old Testament, we do have leaders whom God has put over us. We have pastors, ministers, youth leaders, preachers, Bible study leaders and more. And God takes how we treat our leaders seriously. God has put our leaders over us to lead us for the good of the church and the good of the kingdom. Our leaders are God's leaders, so we need to be treating them accordingly.

When politicians are campaigning for election they spend lots of time talking, meeting people, telling others about their accomplishments, and what they plan on achieving. They do all this to win the respect and trust of the people who are voting for them. Sometimes, if a scandal comes to light, suddenly people lose all respect for them. Respect for leaders is earned by the leaders and it is lost by those same leaders.

However, in the church God gives us a different model to follow. In the church our leaders should have our respect by default because they're God's leaders. If God has put them in a position of authority over us, then we need to respect them. Not because they are any greater than us, but because God is greater than us and he has chosen them to lead us.

1 Thessalonians 5:12-13 says:

> Now we ask you, brothers and sisters, to acknowledge those
> who work hard among you, who care for you in the Lord and

who admonish you. Hold them in the highest regard in love because of their work.

By virtue of the role that our leaders play in our lives we need to respect them. This doesn't mean that you always need to love and agree with everything they do, but certainly we have no right to disrespect them.

Gossiping and Complaining

One really clear application of this means we need to make sure that we aren't gossiping and complaining about those who lead us.

When a leader is doing something we don't like, it can be so easy to vent to someone else we think will understand and agree with us. The problem with this is that as we do it we cement our disrespect of our leaders, we encourage those we are talking to to also dishonour those who lead them, and it poisons the leader's ability to lead.

The first car I ever owned was a big white van. It was actually my family's car, but when I moved out of home my parents generously gave it to me. It was a beautiful car, it had seven seats, a cassette player, and suspicious brown stains on the ceiling. Seeing as it had been the family car for years, I was probably related to the person who caused the stains – it might even have been me. That was an uncomfortable thought. The car was great for driving a lot of people around but terrible for looking cool, impressing women, or just generally functioning as an automobile. The car had been designed with brake pads that were too small, so you had to have them replaced every 10,000km. Whenever I drove around a corner it would let out a sound that was halfway between a lightsaber and a dying cow – "Rwwwwwaaaaaaaooooooowwwwwwww". Often the engine would stall, even though it was an auto – I'd take off at the lights and then the car would die right in the middle of the intersection. It was very embarrassing.

The van would regularly just start steaming. Some pipe would burst and I'd be stuck on the side of the road in the middle of the night. Once, as I was approaching a T-intersection, my brakes failed. I put my foot down on the pedal and nothing happened. Directly in front of me was a cemetery and I was heading straight for it with no brakes. "At least they won't have to take me far to bury me," I thought.

Needless to say, I did not like that car very much. I mean, I had a lot of affection for it, but I spent a lot of time complaining about it. My friends spent a lot of time making fun of me and my car too. I spent a lot of time scheming about how to get rid of my car and upgrade it. When that day finally came it was a liberating experience. I sold it for $200 to a scrap metal dealer. I suspect his friends teased him too.

What does all this have to do with how we treat our leaders? I did not have a lot of respect for my car. My friends did not have much respect for my car. We talked about it behind its back. If a car has a face, we were rude to its face. But none of this stopped the car from being able to do the job of being a car.

Cars don't need respect, it doesn't matter if their reputation gets sullied, or if people gossip about them. Cars need petrol and maintenance and they'll be fine.

But leaders, on the other hand, are different. If we treat leaders with disrespect, if we gossip about them, if we are rude behind their backs or to their faces, it makes it much more difficult for them to do their job. They need support and respect, because leadership is a hard job, and they are people like you and me. There have definitely been leaders over the years whom I have not treated the way I should. I have gossiped about them, and complained and it hasn't helped them or me one little bit. People have done the same to me, and it's hurt, and made life much harder.

This is why we need to respect our leaders, because they are reliant on the people they lead to treat them well, otherwise they can't do their job. When we respect our leaders both in public and privately we make it easy for them to lead. We respect them because they are God's leaders, and our honour for God is reflected in how we treat his leaders.

Respect and Disagreement

So how do we respect our leaders? Well for one, if you're going to gossip, gossip well. We love to talk behind people's backs, so feel free to do it. But say good things about people. If word gets back to the person you're talking about, make sure they're good words. Imagine that? It would be wonderful for your pastor to hear second hand that you've been telling everyone what a good job they've been doing. They'll be chuffed, and they'll be able to do an even better job because they'll feel your support. Being a good gossip is a win for everyone.

Our leaders have a job to do. When we respect and support our leaders we build them up and make a hard job easier to do. Much of what follows is about how we respect our leaders in churches, but a lot of this can also apply to your leaders in the rest of your life too – teachers, principals, bosses, the crossing-guard, Colonel Sanders. God has given you leaders in all sorts of places who deserve your respect. If you don't have church leaders, I'm sure you can figure out how to apply this stuff in other parts of your life.

"Hold on!" you might be saying. "What if I have a problem with my leaders? They're not perfect."

And you'd be right, they're not perfect, but you're not either. So when you have a problem, in my opinion, the first and best thing to do is to suck it up. Chances are, if you're as selfish as me, usually the things that upset us are not actually that big a deal. We don't like the preaching, we don't like the worship, we don't like the sermon, the music's too loud, the music's too soft, there isn't enough ministry for people our age, they're too charismatic, they're not charismatic enough, they're too casual, they're too formal, they're too emotional, they're too clinical and intellectual. And on it goes.

The list of complaints we have in churches about our leaders usually comes from us feeling like our needs aren't met. But you know what, church isn't here to meet our needs. We've been saved by Jesus, our needs have already been met. The church is here to glorify God and grow his kingdom. So if we've got a problem, unless it relates to the glory of God and the growth of his kingdom, we need to stop complaining, and get on with glorifying God and growing his kingdom.

However, say you actually think you've got a legitimate gripe, don't go telling everyone your issues. Go find someone you trust, someone wiser than you, probably older, and not connected to the leader, and who will tell you the truth when they think you're wrong. Tell them what you think and ask them if you actually have something worth being upset about. If they tell you you're complaining about nothing, drop it, and get on with glorifying God and growing his kingdom. If they think your concerns are valid, then it's time to talk to the leader. Don't talk to other people, go straight to the source.

How to Speak

If you do speak to them, do it well. Meet with them respectfully and give them an opportunity to talk. Don't accuse them of wrongdoing, ask them what's going on and then genuinely listen to the answer with a willingness to change your mind. You can imagine if the youths at Bethel had done that, things would have gone very differently. If, instead of just insulting Elisha, one of them had approached him and said, "Elisha, you know here in Bethel we worship the golden calf. Yet you come here and tell us that we should worship Yahweh without statues and that we're breaking God's rules. When you say that

I feel you're attacking something very precious to us here in Bethel, so I'm just wondering why you do that?" Of course, not many teenagers talk that way, but you get the picture. Then, instead of cursing them, Elisha would probably have explained to them the Ten Commandments and why worshipping idols is wrong. No bears would have come out of the woods and everyone would have gone home with their limbs intact.

So if you're going to have a go at a leader, you've got to be very careful how you do it. 1 Timothy 5:19 says, "Do not entertain an accusation against an elder unless it is brought by two or three witnesses." It's saying you need to have the same standards for accusing an elder of wrongdoing as in a court of law. It's a serious thing to publicly accuse our leaders of wrongdoing and we need to treat it as such.

Follow the Leaders

If our leaders are God's leaders then how we respond to them can't just end at respect. If their job is to lead, then our job is to follow. Now obviously I'm not getting this straight from the story of the rampaging bears because none of those boys really did much following, but there certainly is good biblical support for following the leaders God has put over you. It's the natural response to a true leader.

Hebrews 13:17 says, "Have confidence in your leaders and submit to their authority, because they keep watch over you as those who must give an account. Do this so that their work will be a joy, not a burden, for that would be of no benefit to you."

We follow our leaders because they have a job to do and they're the ones who are best equipped to do it. They are the ones out in front. They're taking the risks, they're having the meetings, doing the praying, searching for answers, and making the decisions. They know more about what's happening than we do. Our job is to trust them and follow. If we traipse off on our own, we're gonna get lost and we'll be no help to the church or our leaders.

Sometimes this won't be a problem, because following is easy when you enjoy the direction you're being taken in. It's a lot harder when you don't. But just because you aren't keen, that doesn't mean you get an excuse to not follow. Submitting to our leaders is only impressive when it goes against what we actually want to do.

You may be thinking, some leaders have no idea what they're doing, should I just blindly follow some dumb pastor on some stupid idea, just because I'm told to do it?

For one, if a leader asks you to do something which would be disobedient to God, like firebombing the church down the road, then obviously don't do it. Not even if you think it's a good idea. Your allegiance is to God before your leader.

Furthermore, if your leader wants to do something to you, or someone else, that hurts you or them, you need to tell someone in authority over them. If they are doing something which you know is illegal, you should tell the police. I know that's pretty serious, but sadly some people have used church leadership as a way to exploit or abuse other people and the best thing to do for them, others, and the church, is to tell people who can do something about it, so they can be stopped and helped.

Secondly, if you don't like something you're being asked to do, or don't understand, ask questions. Leaders love getting questions, it shows you're engaging with the life of the church. When you ask, make sure you ask with an attitude of obedience rather than defiance. Ask so that you can serve and follow better, rather than just looking for proof that your leader has a terrible idea.

Paul asked the people of Corinth to follow him, as he followed Christ (see 1 Corinthians 11:1). As far as our leaders represent Christ's authority in the church to us, we need to follow them.

The last thing we can be doing for our leaders is to support them. Of course a big part of our support will come out of our respect and obedience, but there are other things we can do to help our leaders lead well. We can support them in prayer, that they will know God's will, have the strength to do it, and not give in to sin. We can support them by encouraging them and telling them when they've done a good job. Leaders love to hear good feedback. We can support them by getting involved and being enthusiastic. There are not many people who are harder to lead than those who are apathetic. Being an enthusiastic follower is a great way to support our leaders.

Jesus the Great Prophet

In the end none of this is really compelling if it's based purely on the story of some bears attacking some kids. I could perhaps be accused of stretching this point, because while this is a story about how not to respond to leaders, it's not really the comprehensive text on leadership in the Bible. If nothing else, this passage shows us that God takes his prophets seriously. And to reject his prophet is to reject him.

Jesus is God's greatest prophet. He not only spoke for God but was also God himself. In the story of Elisha and the bears we saw that rejection of the prophet caused God's curse to fall on the boys. To reject Christ is to reject God and in doing so we invite God's wrath upon ourselves. When we do not listen to his teaching, or ignore what he did for us at the cross, we reject Jesus. There is no hope for us if we do this. Yet to accept Christ is to accept that Christ has become a curse for us. If we reject God we are cursed, we are headed for death. If we accept Jesus, he takes the curse of sin upon himself. It's as if he gets "mauled" on our behalf, because of our rejection of him, in the process winning us forgiveness and peace with God.

How you treat your leaders should flow not from fear of marauding bears so much as from your love for Jesus, God's greatest prophet. Let's be honest, there is a very small chance you're going to get attacked by a bear for disrespecting your leader. However, for Christ's sake we should serve our leaders well. Christ died for his people, the church, to present us as holy and blameless to God. The Bible even says the church is like Christ's bride, whom he will marry at the end of time (see Ephesians 5:25-33 and Revelation 21). Jesus really loves the church. All of us, leaders and followers, have a role to play in preparing the church for Christ as his pure bride. When you follow your leaders it's part of following Christ. When you respect your leaders, it's part of respecting Christ. When you treat your leaders well, even if you're lovingly disagreeing with them, it's part of honouring Jesus. So follow well, love and support your leaders, because they are God's gift to you to help you grow his kingdom and change this world.

"We were with child, we writhed in labour, but we gave birth to wind." – Isaiah 26:18

8

The Only Fart
in the Bible

Isaiah 26:16-19

A Fart?

I know what you're thinking: "A fart in the Bible? This is too good to be true." I know. But the Bible speaks to everyone, even those of us who think flatulence is hilarious.

Where is this fart you ask? It's in a prophecy in the book of Isaiah.[1]

---

1 While this chapter is titled "The Only Fart in the Bible", there is a very small chance there may in fact be two! There is one very disputed

This prophecy was written by the prophet Isaiah to the people of Judah. Following the death of King Solomon there was a civil war that split Israel in two. Judah was the name of the southern kingdom, the northern kingdom kept the name Israel. Judah had been going through some tough times. Because of their sin the people of Judah had been having increasingly bad relations with foreign powers who were ruling over them and demanding tributes from them. The Assyrians had taken Israel into captivity and now they were breathing down Judah's neck too.

Throughout this whole time God had been trying to bring them back to himself but Judah hadn't been listening. In this passage the prophet looks back at the difficulties life had brought them and how all their pain had been futile.

> LORD, they came to you in their distress;
>   when you disciplined them,
>   they could barely whisper a prayer.
> As a pregnant woman about to give birth
>   writhes and cries out in her pain,
>   so were we in your presence, LORD.
> We were with child, we writhed in labour,
>   but we gave birth to wind.

---

translation of Joshua 15:18 and Judges 1:14 (they're pretty much the same verse) by a dude called G.R. Driver in which a woman farts while sitting on her donkey. There is little evidence that this translation is correct, but it'd be great if it were true (though the donkey may not have been impressed). Google it, it's an interesting read.

> We have not brought salvation to the earth,
>   and the people of the world have not come to life.
> (Isaiah 26:16-18)

Look at that right there: "we gave birth to wind".

There it is! A fart in the Bible!

The first time I was properly made aware of this verse was when I was at Bible college and my lecturer pointed out the fart. My ear pricked up and I read the passage and realised, "Yes! This is an important verse for me to remember!" All these years later, I still hold it close to my heart.

I have done a lot of research into this passage and I have only ever found one other scholar to confirm that this is in fact a fart.[2] I suspect that this is due to the fact that most scholars are writing books for people who preach, teach, lecture, and write high-minded articles about the Bible. Those kinds of people don't like to make fart jokes in their professional life, they save them for their spare time. It's only really youth pastors who are professionally required to seek any and every scatological reference in the Bible. I went to a Bible college for youth ministry so I guess it only makes sense that my lecturer knew it was his duty to point out this nugget of biblical gold (pun intended). I would ask him if he could confirm it for me, but

---

2 That guy was Mark E. Biddle in his book *A Time to Laugh: Humor in the Bible*, Georgia: Smyth & Helwys, 2013, chapter 7 (accessed 27 February 2018). I found one dude who blogged about it, but you can say whatever you want on a blog. I would know, I've got one.

sadly for those of us still on earth, he's with Jesus now, all his Bible questions answered, or far from his mind, irrelevant in the face of God's magnificence. But for those of us still here, I think it's best we just assume it's a fart. I mean, what else could it be?[3]

My Terrible Disease

I have a terrible disease. It's chronic. It's life long. There is no cure. Sometimes people ask me how I can go on praising God through such hardship. I say, "I don't know, I'm just pretty holy I guess." I suspect that one day soon I will be invited to go on an international inspirational speaking tour of the entire world (at least of the USA, because if I'm honest, that's what I really mean by worldwide). What's this disease, you ask? It's called coeliac disease. It means my body can't absorb gluten. Gluten is magic dust from evil wizards that is hidden in wheat, barley, rye, and oats. I can't eat any of those things. I just live on potatoes and rice. It means I can't have bread, cookies, most cereals, or donuts. If I do, I get the poos. If I keep eating gluten, one day I may get cancer. Can you see how this is bad? No donuts for the rest of my life. How can I live without donuts? I'll die without donuts, but I'll die if I eat donuts too! Some days I stand in front of Krispy Kreme and sing that great 80s love song that goes, "I can't live, with or without you."[4]

---

3 Don't answer that. Let's just assume it's a fart, otherwise we'll ruin the fun.

4 Okay, so I'm exaggerating a bit here. I definitely get the poos and I'm more likely to get cancer if I keep eating gluten but it's not automatic. It's a sad world we live in when donuts are a danger to your life. Also

One of the symptoms of coeliac disease is severe bloating. Before I was diagnosed (which was a lot longer than it should have been because I suspected if I went to the doctor they'd tell me I had coeliac disease and I didn't want to know that because donuts) I would often get sick. Sometimes this meant that I would feel a cramp in my abdomen and a tautness in my stomach. I'd think to myself, "Oh no! I'm getting sick!" I'd have visions of being stuck on the toilet for hours on end. The pain would get worse and worse, I couldn't concentrate it hurt so much, I'd have trouble walking. I'd think, "I'd better head to the toilet." And then when I was on my way . . . "Pwwwffffftttttttttffffffftttttttttttt!" I'd let out a giant fart, and it was amazing! I was delivered and set free! Suddenly everything was right in the world again. When that happened it felt like I'd just birthed something, even if it was just gas, a gas baby to bring me joy as it goes into the world and blesses all those it meets.

Birth to Wind

Well this passage is kind of like that, but different. Worse. The image we get of Judah is that they are in great pain. Pain like childbirth. I've never had a baby myself and I don't have any kids. However, everything I know about childbirth seems terrible. There is blood, and screaming, and tearing, and bodily

---

recently a shop in my city started selling gluten-free donuts. They aren't quite as good as real donuts, but for counterfeit donuts, they're pretty darn good. So, you know, there are worse things in life than living without glutenous donuts. Like funnel-web spiders and gluten-free hot dog buns to name just two.

fluids everywhere. I've heard terrible stories, like labour that lasts for days. Why anyone would be willing to have a baby is beyond me. I would encourage every sane woman to consider adoption or a pet fish. Both options require less pain but still bring you the joy of caring for a small creature that will consume your resources, live in your house rent free, and expect you to pay for its education. But nobody ever takes my advice, people keep having babies. I guess all the pain must be worth it, for at the end there is a child, there is joy. There is new life in the world.

For Judah, however, Isaiah is saying we've gone through that pain and striving and it's led to nothing. We've groaned and screamed and cried. We've writhed in distress. We've been through blood, stress, death. Our circumstances have not been good. But at the end, when there should have been joy, when there should have been happiness, when the promise of new life should have come through, there has been nothing. Hot air. Gas. Flatulence. All our striving and suffering have come to nothing.

All their work, all their pain could not save them. They could not bring life to the earth. Everything amounts to nothing.

Hope

But this is not the end. There is a promise. Verse 19 brings hope:

But your dead will live, Lord;
  their bodies will rise—
let those who dwell in the dust
  wake up and shout for joy—
your dew is like the dew of the morning;
  the earth will give birth to her dead.

There will be life, there will be birth. Not the birth of a new baby, but something greater, something more amazing! The earth will give birth to those who have been buried within. God is promising that he will bring resurrection life to the earth. Death, that great enemy, the last thing that defeats us all, will be defeated (see 1 Corinthians 15:51-57). Salvation cannot come from the striving of Judah; it only comes through the work of God!

Our Failure, Our Hope

We can take hold of the promises of this passage for ourselves. No doubt you will face hard times in your life, if you have not faced them already. Times when all your strivings fail, everything you work for turns to dust, your plans amount to nothing but hot air, your relationships are lost to the wind, when the promises of life seem like mere flatulence. We will all have times when we look back and have nothing to show for our efforts, when there is no joy after the pain. We too can feel like Judah. But if we trust in God, we can know that whatever our circumstances are now, if the dead have not yet been raised, the end has not come.

I would like to have some inspiring story to share with you here. Maybe a story about how I overcame hardship, or something bad happened to me but then it turned good.[5] But any story about joy before Jesus' return is a lesser story than the one that is still to be told.

Often in life we set goals for ourselves. We think, "If I can just beat this sin. If I can just date this person. If I can just get this job. If I can just marry this person. If I can just do this good work. If I just pray this prayer. If I just have enough faith. Then I'll be happy. Then I'll be healed. Then I'll be sinless. Then I'll be content. Then I'll be right with God." But when we get what we want or we do what we set out to do, we are still just as unhappy, just as sick, just as sinful, just as lonely, just as far from God as before.

Our culture sells us the lie that we can do anything. We can master our destiny. We can control our own happiness. We deserve our salvation, or at very least we can earn it. We can't.

I once felt called by God to start a new church. There was a lot of excitement amongst Christians at the time about starting

---

5 Once, when I was on a plane with my wife, the flight attendants ignored us because they were talking to some more interesting people across the aisle. When the head flight attendant found out we had been ignored, she was very upset, and gave us business class drinks and a huge bag of M&M's. This is a story of something bad that turned good, but it's not really inspiring enough to make it into the actual book, so you can just get a small amount of inspiration here that my wife and I overcame the odds and received M&M's. God's blessings are good.

new churches, because new churches are pretty much the best way to help people meet Jesus for the first time.

I had this great idea for a church: we'd have a church with three pastors. Each with different gifts and skills (for example, preaching, evangelism, pastoral care, administration, hand-to-hand combat and weaponry, scrapbooking, worship leading, etc.) so that there wasn't just one pastor who had to be good at everything. Each pastor would have equal authority and different responsibilities.

I set about looking for my other two pastors. Eventually I found them; it took me about three years but I did it. Along the way, we also found a place to start the church, a new suburb in north-west Sydney that was about to grow faster than a teenager on steroids (not that teenagers should be on steroids except for prescribed medical purposes - yikes, almost got us all in trouble). And we found some good Jesus-loving people who were moving out to the area and keen to be part of starting the church. Somewhere along the way we started meeting on Sundays in a house near to where the church would be. I moved out to the area, as did another pastor. It was all systems go.

While the church formed itself we gave it the name Gotham City Church. We weren't in Gotham City, I just thought that'd be a super cool name for a church. And I was right, it is a super cool name for a church. When our church start-up group met we called ourselves the Justice League, which was also cool. This was before the *Justice League* movie came out and made us all Marvel fans.

Somewhere along the way the third pastor pulled out. She was, and still is, great, but she realised the model wasn't going to work with her leadership style. It was sad to see her go but she made the hard call at the right time, before things got too far along and leaving was messier.

Not wanting to lose momentum we decided to push on with two pastors and keep looking for a third pastor to complete our tri-pastorate. We continued to meet on Sundays as the Justice League. We were constantly inviting people to come visit us, to see what the church was like and perhaps even join the Justice League. Over the eighteen months we were meeting together as a small church of eight adults and four kids, we invited at least fifty, perhaps a hundred, people to check us out. Lots of them said, "Yes! Sounds great! I'll make sure I visit!" or, "Absolutely. See you on Sunday!" And they never turned up. In a year and a half one person joined the Justice League and that was because I got engaged to her (I could only use that trick once). Other than that we had only one visitor — only one person who managed to turn up — and nothing else.

We were supernaturally bad at starting a church. More people have visited the moon than visited my church.

Eventually, the other pastor and I decided to pull the plug. We shut down the church so that all the great people we had in our church could go and serve in other churches where they could be more helpful to the work of God. We all left the church as friends, but it was pretty sad to see this church we had been working on for years end in nothing. All the work we had put in, all the plans we made, all the sacrifices and house moves, and dreams dreamt, amounted to nothing.

Sometimes our stories end in failure. Sometimes we don't see victory. Sometimes cancer wins, families stay broken, we fail our exams, or our friends abandon us and they never come back. Sometimes the story doesn't end well. What we thought would save us, doesn't. Death still infects every part of life.

And that's the point. After all Judah's striving they had nothing to show for it. Judah thought that if they worked hard, if they suffered, if they endured the hardships inflicted upon them, they would overcome. Surely in the end they would bring "salvation". Surely through their efforts they could bring new life. But they couldn't and they didn't.

And neither can we bring ourselves life. Neither can we save ourselves from the death that is in everything.

Around 700 years after this passage was written there was one from the tribe of Judah who did bring new life, Jesus Christ. In him we see the solution to the problem, the defeater of death. In his death and resurrection we see the end of the story.

There is hope, but it is not found in our striving, or in our labour. We do not bring salvation to the earth. Salvation has come to us in the Son of God. When we trust in him, we can experience new life. Our sin is forgiven. Little by little, death is expelled from us, and life takes hold. Though the world around us wastes away, inwardly we are being renewed day by day (see

2 Corinthians 4:16).

One day Jesus will return and put everything right. All who have trusted in him will be raised to life. Death will be destroyed. We will have resurrection bodies just like the one Jesus had, and still has, when he rose from the tomb. Then we will live forever in God's perfect new creation. When we grasp this truth it puts everything else in perspective.

When our church failed it was painful, but knowing that Jesus was in charge was enough. I don't have to be successful, my plans don't always have to come together. Knowing that I was called to be faithful and I could trust Jesus with the outcome was enough. Jesus loves me no matter how well I do. If I keep failing for the rest of my life, he'll keep loving me. That's pretty comforting to know.

Many stories end in failure, but in the great story, our God has succeeded on our behalf. We may not see victory now, but Jesus' victory will one day override all that now holds us back. Cancer may win, but it has not won – that honour belongs to our Saviour. Families may break apart, but God welcomes us into an eternal heavenly family. We can fail our exams, but Christ is our success, we are more than our failures. Our friends may abandon us, but our God would not leave us in our sin, nor will he abandon us in life or death. Some stories don't end well, but the great story will. What we thought would save us, doesn't, but the rejected, abandoned, broken man on the cross, turns out to be the creator of the universe dying for the sins of the world. Death still infects every part of life, but one day death will be destroyed, the world will be remade, hot air gives way to new life, the earth will give birth to her dead and we will live forever. The story isn't over. Wake up and shout for joy!

9

Ezekiel the Poo Chef

Ezekiel 4:1-17

Crazy Illustrations

There are plenty of preachers in the world who love a good, theatrical illustration.

I once pretended to get drunk while preaching. I had a bottle of Jack Daniels (filled with apple juice) which I sipped from as I took suggestions from the church about what they'd like to add to church services to make them more appealing. I don't remember many of the suggestions, except for the guy who suggested scantily clad cheerleaders, cheering for Jesus. By pretending to be drunk I was attempting to illustrate how inappropriate Israel's behaviour was when they were worshipping false gods. I'm not sure how successful I was. Perhaps, fittingly, it was all just an inappropriate mess.

I once attended a youth event where the preacher started to take her clothes off as she preached. I was there with my youth group, and I spent the whole illustration stressing about what I was going to have to tell their parents when they found out I took their kids to a worship event that turned into a strip show. When the preacher finally stopped (she was down to her unrevealing underwear), saying she couldn't continue for reasons of child protection, I literally breathed a sigh of relief. The fourteen-year-old boy behind me, on the other hand, let out an audible cry of disappointment. No doubt, up until that point the kid thought it was the greatest sermon of all time. I think the sermon was about being real before God in our worship.

Some preachers take it even further. When I was a teenager, one of my friends had a father who was a pastor. Once while preaching he took his shirt off and preached the rest of the sermon topless, and he wasn't even at the beach. While he probably just looked like your average pasty, white Anglican preacher, I like to imagine that he looked like The Rock and the sermon was about God giving us the strength of a mighty warrior. When I look like The Rock I intend to preach topless most of the time too. I will serve as a walking illustration of the beauty of God's creation.

Chances are, if you've been around preachers for a while you'll have come across a crazy illustration or two. When a preacher does one of these illustrations they will explain why they just did what they did and everyone will nod and say, "Ahh, I see. Great illustration." Or perhaps, "What? I don't see how that connects, why are we talking about having cheerleaders in church and why is my youth pastor pretending to be drunk?"

Sign-Acts and Crazy Artists

In this passage from Ezekiel we see Ezekiel the prophet doing what is known as a "sign-act". A sign-act is an enacted prophecy that illustrates for the people of Israel something of what God is doing, or will do among them. Throughout Ezekiel chapter 4 we read about how Ezekiel spent over a year doing these sign-acts and he didn't even get to explain them. They were a silent witness to how God was judging his people. The people watching his antics wouldn't have been able to figure out what was going on till some later date.

In the art world there are a bunch of different disciplines that an artist can work in. Some paint, some draw, some make sculptures, and some take photos. Some, probably the craziest ones, are performance artists. These artists are the ones who use their bodies to perform some strange thing and then everyone watching has to figure out exactly why they're doing what they're doing. For instance, one pregnant artist gave birth to her child in a museum, another artist lived inside a dead bear for two weeks, and another artist sat at a table with a bunch of objects including a feather, some grapes, a whip, a rose, a knife, and a gun and allowed the audience to interact with her using the objects however they wished, for good or bad. All these artists had something to say but it wasn't immediately apparent; you had to watch, you had to think, you had to read a statement by the artist or hear them speak about it later. It's only by seeking the answer that you can actually understand the significance of what's happening; otherwise it's just a strange person doing weird stuff.

Ezekiel and many of the other Old Testament prophets are the performance artists of the Bible. God asks them to perform some strange sign-act so that Israel may not just hear God's truth but will also see it. They are perhaps the forerunners of Christ, who is the ultimate sign-act. In his life, death, and resurrection we see the truth of God's character, love, judgement, and mercy enacted within the physical life of God himself.

So what is going on in Ezekiel 4? In this series of four sign-acts (we see the last one in Ezekiel 5) God asked Ezekiel to perform a series of actions that showed what he was doing and what was going to happen to the people of Israel.

In the first one God asked Ezekiel to "take a block of clay, put it in front of you and draw the city of Jerusalem on it" (v. 1). Then he was asked to "erect siege works against it, build a ramp up to it, set up camps against it and put battering rams around it" (v. 2). This was to symbolise the coming siege of Jerusalem. Ezekiel was then to take an iron pan, place it in front of the tablet, and besiege the model Jerusalem. Ezekiel was to play the role of God. This sign-act was showing that God himself was going to besiege Jerusalem. He wasn't coming to save them – this was his judgement.

This first sign is a little strange, but not abnormal. There are many men who love building models in their spare time. This sign is like that, only when you build a model train set in your garage you're not doing it to tell people about the judgement of God, you're just telling people you need more friends.

In the next sign, after Ezekiel had laid siege to a model Jerusalem, God asked him to lie on his left side for 390 days, then on his right side for forty days. This time Ezekiel was representing the people of Israel and Judah, bearing their sin, one day for each year that they had been sinning against God (see vv. 4-8).

Cooking with Poo

Now comes the third sign. Throughout this period Ezekiel was to live on a starvation diet, where each day he was to cook for himself a small amount of bread and eat it while drinking a small amount of water.

And then here comes the kicker. God asked Ezekiel to "bake it in the sight of the people, using human excrement for fuel" (v. 12). God was asking Ezekiel to do a poo, make it into a fire, then cook his food on it. Or as some commentators suggest, cook the bread in the poo, because that's how bread was baked – right inside the fire.

Can you imagine how Ezekiel must have been feeling?

> God: Make a clay picture of Jerusalem.

> Ezekiel: No problem.

> God: Lay siege to it.

> Ezekiel: I'll feel a bit silly, but okay.

> God: Lie on your side for over a year, then roll over and lie on the other side for another month and a bit.

> Ezekiel: Really? I guess . . . if you want.

> God: Each day eat a really small amount of food.

> Ezekiel: Man, this just gets worse and worse. But fine. I am a servant of the Lord.

> God: Each day collect your poo and cook your meals in it.

> Ezekiel: . . .

> God: Ezekiel?

> Ezekiel: . . .

```
God: . . .


Ezekiel: This sucks.
```

Now Ezekiel didn't actually just take this lying down (pun intended). At this point he raised an objection. What amazes me is that it's the cooking with poo that tips him over the edge. I would have objected way before that. I would have objected probably at the point that I was laying siege to a crude drawing of a city on a brick. I'm terrible at drawing. But it takes much longer for Ezekiel to snap. It's like God was trolling Ezekiel just to see how far he could push him. And when Ezekiel did snap it wasn't because he thought poo bread was going to taste disgusting. It was because he was worried it would make him unclean, he would be breaking the Old Testament's cleanliness laws. He didn't want to obey God on this point because it would mean disobeying God on another point. Look at what he said in verse 14: "Not so, Sovereign LORD! I have never defiled myself. From my youth until now I have never eaten anything found dead or torn by wild animals. No impure meat has ever entered my mouth."

Ezekiel's concern was his spiritual purity, not the idea of eating poo-laced bread. Or at least that's the argument he thought would be most persuasive to God. It turns out God was persuaded and relents.

God said, "Very well . . . I will let you bake your bread over cow dung instead of human excrement" (v. 15).

Good guy God, being super flexible and all. I bet Ezekiel was feeling pretty chuffed that he won that battle.

```
Ezekiel: No poo! That's where I draw the
line.

God: Okay. Not man poo, cow poo.

Ezekiel: Better.
```

I saw a video a few years ago about a charity that was making stoves for people in developing nations to burn dried animal dung in so that they could cook with a readily available fuel source. So it seems like animal dung isn't such a bad cooking tool after all. And notice that Ezekiel was allowed to bake the bread "over" the cow dung rather than in it. So with that victory under his belt, he got on with performing the sign-act. Its purpose was to show the God's people what their life would be like when they met his judgement: their food supply would be scarce and defiled. God was saying:

> I am about to cut off the food supply in Jerusalem. The people will eat rationed food in anxiety and drink rationed water in despair, for food and water will be scarce. They will be appalled at the sight of each other and will waste away because of their sin. (vv. 16-17)

Things weren't looking so good for Judah. For those who were willing to hear the message, I suspect it wasn't a message they wanted to hear.

Bearing Bad News

There is definitely a challenge for us in this passage. God asked Ezekiel to tell Israel an unpleasant truth. I suspect none of them really wanted to hear about how God was going to besiege them, how they were sinful, how they were going to pay the penalty for their sins. No one would have seen this sign-act, heard the interpretation and then said, "Wow! Thanks, Ezekiel! What an encouragement!" No one would have been inviting Ezekiel to their dinner parties in case he spent the whole night warning them of impending judgement, or he lay on their living room floor for the next year. Generally people get upset when you tell them bad news, especially if it reflects badly on their character. I rarely go to the dentist because I suspect they are going to tell me I have gum disease and cavities all due to my poor flossing technique and hidden lust issues. I'd prefer not to have a dentist look into my mouth and judge my soul, so I stay well away.

Poor Ezekiel had an unpleasant truth to share, and he had to share it in an unpleasant way. Sometimes when God gives his people a message to share, it's not a good message and the telling of the message is not always an enjoyable process. If you're a Christian then God has given you the very best message to share. You get to tell people that God loves them, and that he has made a way for them to spend eternity with him. This is great news! The difficult part is that before you tell the really good news, you have to share some really bad news.

The really bad news of the gospel is that we are all people who have sinned against God, we are all facing his judgement and if we do not repent we will be punished for our sins with eternal death. That's about as bad as news gets. If you tell someone who thinks they're doing pretty well that a) they actually aren't doing pretty well, b) God is angry at them because c) they aren't nearly as good as they thought they were, they may not take the news very well, and they may take it out on you even if you are just passing on the message of the Bible.

When I speak about the Bible I feel the weight of responsibility very strongly, especially if I'm speaking to a bunch of people who don't believe the Bible like I do. There is always the temptation just to tell the good bits, or to water down the difficult bits. I once heard a talk all about how Jesus saves us, and instead of talking about our sin the preacher talked about our brokenness as if sin is merely something that has happened to us, rather than something that we have actively chosen to participate in. I know that I have sometimes described sin as "poor choices" because "evil choices" sounds too harsh. It's easier, and less offensive, to talk about brokenness and poor choices rather than sin.

Of course we are broken because other people have hurt us, and sometimes we stuff things up because we are dumb rather than depraved, but the Bible won't let us leave it at that. Not when it says that "Jews and Gentiles alike are all under the power of sin" (Romans 3:9), that "all have sinned and fall short of the glory of God" (Romans 3:23), and that even our "righteous acts are like filthy rags" (Isaiah 64:6). It's difficult to escape the bad news of the Bible.

What's more, the punishment for that sin is not good news either. The punishment is death, and not just like slipping off quietly in your sleep. It's the eternal death of being sent to hell for eternity. Sometimes people call hell "the absence of God". I know I've described it like that in the past. But even that is sugar-coating it; hell is the active punishment of God. Hell is not the absence of God; it's the just presence of God's wrath. Revelation tells us that "Anyone whose name [is] not found written in the book of life [will be] thrown into the lake of fire" (Revelation 20:15), and Jesus describes hell as "the eternal fire prepared for the devil and his angels" (Matthew 25:41). Hell is clearly created by God so that he might use it as his primary instrument of judgement.

The final bit of bad news is that this judgement from God is coming. One way or another all of us are going to stand before Jesus and face judgement. God "will judge the world with justice by the man he has appointed" (Acts 17:31). If we haven't trusted in Jesus we will be punished for our lives of sin. This includes all people, from the richest to the poorest, from the people you hate to the people you love. Apart from Jesus, no one escapes the judgement of God.

This doesn't sound like good news, and we can't escape it. Jesus didn't try to make it sound better than it was, nor did he apologise or shy away from God's wrath, and neither should we. Now this doesn't mean that every time you want to talk about Jesus you have to start by saying, "Hi, how are you? Let me tell you about hell!" Chances are, if you do that, no one will hang around for the good bit. While often the prophets like Ezekiel started with doom, Jesus had many different ways of sharing the good news of God's kingdom. Sometimes he healed people, or did miracles. Sometimes he told stories. In today's world people can begin to understand who God is and what he has done without chronologically first hearing about God's wrath. Sometimes seeing the good news of what God has done in someone's life, or recognising the goodness of Jesus, can draw us in to discovering more about God's story. Sometimes discovering everything we need to know, good and bad, can take a long time, months or even years. However, none of this means we should neglect to share the truth of our situation before God. We have to be honest about the bad news. Only when we understand what we have done, what we deserve, and what we are bound for, can we fully appreciate the grace and mercy of God in Jesus. And not until we can grasp, even to a small degree, the severity of God's wrath can we begin to comprehend how much Jesus went through on our behalf when he suffered that same wrath at the cross. Understanding the bad news means we can love and respond to the good news. The good news – hang in there, we've almost got to it - grows ever more wonderful the more we understand how terrible the bad news is.

To pass on this message of bad then good news isn't exactly enjoyable. It's not quite lying on your side for a year, or cooking your food on poo, but it isn't going to feel exactly comfortable either. People will not thank you for telling them that their behaviour has them bound for hell, and that they face the wrath of an angry God. This is not a comfortable message. Comfort, however, is not what we're saved for. Jesus doesn't command us to live a comfortable life. In fact, Jesus promises the exact opposite (see John 15:20) – following him is going to be rough and we're not going to win many friends (see Matthew 10:34-39).

The Really, Really Good News

In spite of all of this, the good news we share is really, really good news. It's the best news! God hasn't left us without hope. We have a saviour and he has taken God's wrath upon himself. Jesus took our bad news—he took the punishment that we deserve—so that we might get only good news. And this news is not just that God forgives us but he loves us so much that he welcomes us into his family. We become his adopted children. How great that the God of the universe loves us so much that he would pick us to be in his royal family? I rarely got picked for sports teams at school, yet God wants to be my father forever!

But there's even more. This news isn't just for individuals, it's for the whole world. One day Jesus is coming back and he's going to remake the world so that it's the way it should be, so that it's better than it's ever been. He'll put an end to evil and injustice and make earth a place where "there will be no more death or mourning or crying or pain" (Revelation 21:4). And Jesus isn't going to just change the world in the future, he is changing us now! All the things that we get wrong, all the ways we're broken and sinful now, he is at work in us, little by little, bit by bit, to be more like him. This is good news. And that's just the beginning of it.

How great is this news? If anyone trusts in Jesus they can be saved from hell and have eternal life in his new creation with the God who loves them and saved them into his family. This means that the good news we share is not just good news in general, like finding out that your favourite team has won the Grand Final, but good news for you personally, like finding out there is a life-saving treatment available for your cancer. The good news is life-saving news, so we must share it so that everyone might have the opportunity to have their life changed from bad news to good news, by the work of Jesus.

What this *doesn't* mean is that you can use the bad news (true as it may be) as an excuse to have a go at all those people you don't like. The truth of God's wrath is not an excuse to relish the judgement of God, or take a perverse joy in the punishment of those who haven't been as "smart" as you and got themselves saved. Jesus was heart broken at the thought of his fellow Jews' refusal to trust in God (see Matthew 23:37). Our hearts should be the same. We aren't saved because of our own smarts or righteousness, it is entirely by God's grace; we have no reason to boast and no reason to think we're any better than anyone else (see Ephesians 2:1-10). Let's not get too full of ourselves, were it not for God's decision to call us to himself, the bad news of those who haven't trusted in Jesus would be our bad news too. In fact, their bad news *is* our bad news, because how can we be content while our friends, family, and fellow humans are still bound by sin and darkness?

The life lived in obedience to God doesn't promise "fun times for all". We only have to look at the life of Jesus to know that obedience will lead to our death before it will lead to our glory. Jesus spoke an uncompromising truth, and it got him killed. Our commitment to making God's truth known, so that his good news might be believed, and people might be saved, will be uncomfortable, but it may also lead to salvation for those who hear. Wouldn't it be great if we were known for following in the footsteps of Ezekiel and speaking truth even if the message is hard and the telling hurts? So get on with your truth telling and thank God that he's not making you cook with poo . . . yet.

"She lusted after her lovers, whose genitals were like those of donkeys and whose emission was like that of horses." – Ezekiel 23:20

10

Ezekiel's Porn

Ezekiel 23:19-21

Genitals and Emissions

Sometimes when Christians write encouraging notes to each other they'll write a reference for a Bible verse at the end of their note. It'll say something like, "Keep trusting Jesus! Jeremiah 29:11" or, "God loves you more than you know! John 3:16." Sometimes when Christians want to be funny they'll write something like, "You're the best! Ezekiel 23:19-21." And then the poor person, seeking a little bit of encouragement, will look up the passage and read:

> Yet she became more and more promiscuous as she recalled the days of her youth, when she was a prostitute in Egypt. There she lusted after her lovers, whose genitals were

> like those of donkeys and whose emission was like that of
> horses. So you longed for the lewdness of your youth, when
> in Egypt your bosom was caressed and your young breasts
> fondled.

If they have a similar sense of humour they'll laugh, otherwise they might get offended at the pornographic language of the Bible.

As a young kid I remember sitting in my Christian primary school and when we were bored this was one of those verses we would turn to. In the same way that the first thing I did in school when I got a new art textbook or science textbook was look for the naked pictures, or how every time I got my hands on a calculator I would key in "5318008" and then turn it upside down, Ezekiel 23:19-21 was one of the go-to passages for a good, immature giggle. I would laugh, "Genitals like donkeys and emissions like horses! So funny!" I didn't even know what emissions were, I just knew they were disgusting! Recently in Australian politics there was a lot of debate over an Emissions Trading Scheme. Now that I'm a grown up I know they aren't talking about the same sort of emissions. Or at least I hope they're not because that would be disgusting and do nothing for the environment.

I think perhaps, as a ten-year-old, this was not the kind of stuff I should have been reading. It's pretty darn explicit. As a thirty-five-year-old I feel like I still shouldn't be reading it. So why would Ezekiel just casually drop a little bit of hard-core porn in the Bible?

Shocking

If reading this passage leaves you feeling shocked then you have entirely the right response. You're meant to be shocked, this is meant to be shocking language. Nowhere else in the Bible is there anything quite as explicit as this. There is Song of Songs, which is pretty explicit, but most of the language is poetic so if you don't think about it too much you can tell yourself that most of it is just about a guy who's really enthusiastic about pomegranates. Ezekiel isn't being discreet at all here. You can't read "genitals like that of donkeys" without getting a rather unpleasant picture in your head of exactly that. Unless you have no idea what a donkey's genitals look like, in which case you're probably better off.

So why would Ezekiel do this? Why would he want to shock his readers with all this talk of emissions and breast fondling?

As you can probably tell from the way it is written Ezekiel isn't trying to write some steamy, biblical romance. This is harsh language. While as a kid I only read those few verses in isolation, if you really want to understand what's going on you have to understand the whole chapter these verses are in and the context in which they were written. Unfortunately things are way less funny when you read them in context.

When God's people became a nation, after escaping from Egypt and wandering in the desert, they came into the land that God had promised to Abraham. After spending a while fighting wars, they took control of the land, and eventually became the kingdom of Israel. Their capital city was Jerusalem. This is where God was worshipped and his temple was built. For a while in Israel things went okay, not great, but okay. However, after King Solomon's reign his son, Rehoboam, became king. All the people asked him to be a kind king, but, listening to the advice of his stupid friends, Rehoboam declared, "My father made your yoke heavy; I will make it even heavier. My father scourged you with whips; I will scourge you with scorpions" (1 Kings 12:14). One wonders how easy it is to use scorpions as whips, but I suspect he was just being poetic. Plus it sounds scarier to scourge someone with a scorpion, than if you promise to scourge them with even worse whips than the whips they have previously been scourged with.

The people of Israel didn't much like the idea of being hit with mean insects so they rebelled against Rehoboam. Of the twelve tribes of Israel, ten of them split off and formed their own kingdom with a new king, Jeroboam, and a new capital city, Samaria. These ten tribes became known as the northern kingdom of Israel, and the remaining two tribes who stuck with Rehoboam (and his scorpions) became the southern kingdom of Judah.

The northern kingdom never had a good king, they never had a king who properly worshipped the true God, Yahweh. They were always finding other gods to worship. What's more, instead of trusting God for their protection, they decided to trust in another nation to look after them. When the Assyrians came and invaded, they decided to pay them a bunch of money so they wouldn't attack them. It was kinda like paying the mafia not to burn down your salami shop. God wasn't too impressed though, he wanted kings who obeyed him and a nation that trusted him, so when he had had enough he sent the Assyrians in to destroy them. Ironically, the people they looked to for protection destroyed them. The entire country was taken over, the people of Israel were taken into captivity and scattered across the Assyrian empire. The northern kingdom of Israel never existed again.

Oholah and Oholibah

Now in our passage Ezekiel is speaking to the southern kingdom of Judah, and they're probably pretty pleased with themselves. They're so much more holy than those evil northerners were. Ezekiel, as he was saying when he was lying on his side and cooking with poo (see Chapter 9), is telling them that hard times are going to come; God's judgement is on its way in the form of a foreign army who is going to attack them. Chances are the people of Judah don't think they deserve this kind of treatment from God, so in chapter 23, Ezekiel retells their story to them in an allegory - the story of two sisters, Oholah and Oholibah. Oholah represents Israel, the northern kingdom, and her younger sister, Oholibah, represents Judah, the southern kingdom.[1]

---

1 Ezekiel 23:4 says, "Oholah is Samaria, and Oholibah is Jerusalem." Samaria was the capital of Israel and Jerusalem was the capital of Judah. When the passage refers to the capital cities it is using them to represent the whole of the nation, in the same way these days news reporters might talk about Washington DC to refer to the USA or Canberra to refer to

Their story begins in Egypt (where the people of Israel were enslaved before God rescued them) where Oholah and Oholibah become prostitutes. There their "breasts were fondled and their virgin bosoms caressed"[2] (Ezekiel 23:3). We find out that not only are these sisters prostitutes they are also God's two sister wives (see Ezekiel 23:4-5)! Now before you get worried that God has two wives and they're sisters, remember this is all allegory, and every allegory falls down at some point. Allegories are stories to illustrate a deeper point, they aren't going to line up in every detail. In the Bible one of the ways God's relationship to his people is represented is that of a husband to his wife. Seeing as Oholah and Oholibah represent Israel and Judah respectively, they were one country when they were in Egypt, so for the allegory to be truly correct they would have to be one person in Egypt and then at some point, by a miracle of science or some form of dark magic, split into two people, with suddenly separate wills and separate desires, but both still married to the same husband who has suddenly become a bigamist! I suspect Ezekiel chose to make them two separate women from the start because the alternative was

---

Australia (For example, "Tensions between Washington and Canberra have risen this week after the President misunderstood a compliment the Prime Minister paid to the First Lady's thongs").

2 Daniel Block translates this verse, "There they let their breasts be squeezed and there their virgin nipples were fondled." It's not exactly the most eloquent writing but as you can see many translations are tame compared to what it could be (Daniel L. Block, *The Book of Ezekiel, Chapters 1-24*, Grand Rapids: Wm. B. Eerdmans, 1997, pp. 732-733).

too confusing and would probably have distracted from the point he was trying to make: that God's people were like his wife, and while he was faithful to them, they were unfaithful to him, pursuing other gods and seeking the protective strength of other nations.

You probably know what happens next, Israel escape their captivity in Egypt, but that doesn't improve things. Oholah continues to prostitute herself. When she is approached by the Assyrians, she gives herself to them, sleeping with all their high officials. She continues to cheat on her husband, happily sleeping with anyone who wants her. Eventually God gives her fully to the Assyrians, she is no longer under his protection, and she is stripped naked and murdered by the people who were once her lovers. You can read about this in 2 Kings 17.

Seeing what happened to her older sister should have been a lesson to Oholibah. It should have spurred her on to faithfulness to her husband. Instead, she too prostitutes herself to the Assyrians, but she doesn't stop there, she goes even further than her sister. She sees a painting of some Babylonian men on a wall and wants them too. So she sends them a message inviting them into her bed, and they come to her and sleep with her (see Ezekiel 23:14-17).

Eventually God rejects her too, but Oholibah's rejection does not cause her to turn back to God. Instead she thinks back to her days in Egypt, she thinks of them not with remorse but with longing. Longing for the men who have become, in her memory, not even human, but like animals to satisfy her

145

depraved longings, hence Ezekiel 23:19-21 with its donkey genitals and horse emissions. So, like her older sister, God hands her over to her former lovers, and she will endure the consequences of her unfaithfulness.[3]

"That Wasn't Very Funny"

You might be thinking, "That wasn't very funny." Which is true. It's a pretty terrible story. Verses 19-21 are not really very funny at all when you read them in context. The whole of Ezekiel 23 is shocking for its depravity and violence. But, as I said before, the whole point is to shock you. It was written to make the reader sit up and take notice, to ask, "Why would Ezekiel be talking like this?" Ezekiel wanted his audience to know that they were

---

3 I had a wise friend mention to me that they were disappointed that while there are many bits of the Bible that build women up (Rahab, Deborah, Esther, and Ruth in the Old Testament, and Mary (Jesus' mother), Mary and Martha (Jesus' friends), the woman who anointed Jesus' feet, the women who supported Jesus' ministry, the women who were partners in the sharing of the gospel, and more) they don't often feature in parts of the Bible that are weird, crude, funny, or nude. This means that we get a rather skewed version of biblical women in this book. Most passages in this book aren't about women, and if women do feature they are having sex with angels, farting, or prostituting themselves out. There wasn't a good solution to this, so all I can say is, let me encourage you to go read about those women listed above. The Bible has plenty of smart, brave, and godly women, as well as flawed, scared, and sinful women, and everything in between. The more you read the Bible the more you discover how real the Bible is about all of us, whatever our gender, all of us who are loved, valuable, sinful, broken, and in desperate need of Jesus.

heading for the same fate as their sister country to the north. Judah had not been any more holy than Israel, they had been worse! They were going to receive God's punishment, because instead of being faithful to him, they had sought comfort and protection in other nations. He should have been their comfort and protection, but instead they looked to the Assyrians, to the Babylonians, and to the Egyptians. When their punishment came, when the Babylonians came to take them from their land and into captivity, when they were weeping by the waters of Babylon, they would not have the option of pretending they had been hard done by. If they listened to Ezekiel, they would know that their exile and captivity were the logical end point of trusting in anything other than the faithfulness of their God. Ezekiel told a shocking story so that his audience might understand their shocking reality.

What's our Story?

If Ezekiel was to tell our story, what story would he tell? Are we equally deluded? Do we believe things between us and God are great even though we're being unfaithful? Are we running after false gods, or trusting in other people or other things for our security and comfort? I suspect that you are not currently paying tribute to another nation in exchange for protection from possible invasion. However, while our unfaithfulness to God might not look exactly like Judah's did, we can be equally unfaithful in our own lives. Are we trusting in God and God alone or are we prostituting ourselves out to money, or sex, or romance, or popularity, to give us what we can only truly find in God?

The answer to this question can sometimes be difficult to know. It's easy to take a quick inventory of your life and conclude, "Nothing to worry about here. I'm doing fine." In Judah's own self-diagnostics I suspect they would have been happy to report that they were doing well. So how can you know if you trust something else for what only God can give you? How can you and I avoid Judah's delusion? Perhaps a little prayerful imagination will work. Pray and ask God to show you where you might be misplacing your trust and devotion, then run through all the important things in your life and ask yourself, "Would I still be okay if I lost that?" Would you still be okay if all your friends turned on you? Would you still be okay if you lost whatever money you make? Would you still be okay if the person you love left you? Would you still be okay if you were in an accident and were horribly disfigured or unable to walk again? Hopefully none of these things will happen to you, but sometimes it's only after you lose something that you understand how much you were relying on it for your identity and security.

When I run through those questions I know I feel challenged. I know I worry that if I had no job, God wouldn't provide for me, even though I also know that God has always provided for me when I have had no job and no money in the past. I constantly forget that he is my provider, I think that I am my own provider and that it's up to me to make sure I'm okay. That tells me something about where my trust lies. What's more, I know that having a job gives me a sense of identity. I like people knowing that I earn money. I don't need to be rich, but I want people to know that I don't bludge off the government or other people's generosity. I want people to know that I'm valuable to someone. If I lost my job, I worry what people would think of me. I recently had to leave a job and I worried that people would think it was because I was unable to do the job. I wanted people to see things from my perspective and know that the problem wasn't with me. That tells me that my identity lies not in God and his love for me, or the value he places on me, but in the role I play and the way other people see me.

What do you discover when you ask those questions? What do you discover when you contemplate losing the things you love and value? What are you tempted to trust in more than God? What things or people are you trusting to give you what only God can and should give you?

What Do You Do Now?

When you've answered these first questions, the next question is, what should you do about it? Should you end the relationship that you're looking to for meaning and purpose? Should you quit the job that brings you security? Should you stop working out, or stop doing your hair and putting on make-up to avoid the temptation to find your value in your appearance? Should you stop having sex because you're looking to sex to give you ultimate happiness or self-worth? To be honest, I don't know! I don't know your situation, so any kind of blanket advice could be dangerous.[4]

---

4 Actually, that's not true, I think there is some blanket advice I can give: A light cotton blanket will be good in summer, but make sure you have a thick woollen one available for those extra chilly winter nights.

However, there is some advice I can give that should apply to anyone who follows Jesus: if whatever you are looking to for your security and identity is sinful (that is, the Bible teaches that you shouldn't do it) you should stop. Sin not only displeases God, but it hurts you and affects others. Beyond that, I can't say exactly what you should and shouldn't do. Maybe you should break up with that person, maybe you should stop going to the gym. Or maybe you can seek God to help you transform that relationship, and maybe you can figure out how to work out for God's glory. I suspect the answer will be different for different people, in different situations, and at different times.

Let me tell you about what happened with me and my job. I left a job that was the highest paying job I've ever had.[5] When I was looking for a new one, I was only seriously looking at jobs that paid the same or more. I got concerned that I wouldn't be able to survive with less money when I felt like I was only scraping by before. When I was praying and seeking God on what to do, I felt him say to me not to choose a job for the money, that I hadn't been trusting in him and that he would provide. When he told me that, it made looking for jobs easier. I was free to look for something that would best honour him and build his kingdom, rather than just choose the job that would mean I could feel comfortable and secure. In the end, I took a job that paid less, but I have seen God provide time and time again.

---

5 It was a ministry job, so it wasn't heaps of money, but it was money. I'm used to getting paid in Lindt chocolate and thank you cards, so any money is pretty exciting!

It's been so much better for my faith in God to see him come through on his promise to provide than if I had taken a job that paid more and I felt like I had sorted it all out myself. I still worry about money, but I also can remind myself of God's promises in the Bible to care for his people and remember how I have seen that in my life. I suspect until I am resurrected like Jesus I will always be tempted to seek money for security when I should be seeking God, but I know that God will also keep helping me trust him more and more.

God has the answer to your particular situation. As you pray, read the Bible and reflect on those things you are trusting instead of him, and the answer should become clear. It may also be a good idea to chat to an older and wiser Christian who can help you figure out what you should be doing. And once you know what you should do, do it. Usually the hardest part is not knowing what to do, but actually doing it. However, you must do it. In the case of Judah, God had shocking words for them about their behaviour because they didn't understand the real truth of their reality. Because they never understood, God had to use harsh and terrible means, the invasion of a foreign army and their exile from their homeland, so that they might see the depths of their sin and turn back to him.

We can look at what Jesus did for us. The killing of God's son was the most shocking and depraved event in the history of the world but it was the only thing that would bring us back to him. It shows us both the depth of our sin, and the love and trustworthiness of God. Let that be your motivation.

God must be your only security, the only one in whom you place your trust, the only place you find life and value. Seek God's gentle words to you and obey them now so that he will not need to use shocking words and terrible means to bring you to faithfulness later.

"The earth shook, the rocks split and the tombs broke open. The bodies of many holy people who had died were raised to life." – Matthew 27:51-52

11

Matthew's Zombies

Matthew 27:51-53

Jesus Christ the Satan Slayer and Demon Destroyer

Let me confess, the title of this chapter is a little deceptive. I know what you were hoping for. You were hoping for some previously hidden bit of the Bible where actual, real-life zombies came out of their graves and went around eating people's brains. Maybe Jesus and the disciples would go out and destroy a few zombies. Wouldn't it be cool to see Jesus toting a shotgun, Peter holding a crossbow, Thomas with a bloodied baseball bat. And then it wouldn't even upset the whole "love your enemies" thing because how can the undead actually be your enemies? They're just walking corpses.

If there's anything that books such as *Pride and Prejudice and Zombies* prove, it's that adding zombies to a classic will not diminish it in the slightest. If anything, it might even make it better. If only Matthew decided to employ that nugget of literary truth when writing his book.

Sadly, God in his infinite wisdom didn't feel like the Bible needed any extra zombie-exterminating pizzazz. So if Jesus and the disciples did get up to any zombie hunting it's left in the darkness of unrecorded history. We'll just have to satisfy ourselves with Jesus Christ the Satan Slayer and Demon Destroyer instead, which is actually pretty darn awesome, and exactly what we get in this passage in Matthew 27.

The following story, while it may not be full of the flesh-eating undead, does have previously dead people walking around casually saying "Hi" to people. Imagine that:

> Bible Woman: Ohmigoodness! A zombie! Don't eat my brains!
>
> Previously Dead Person: Actually, ma'am, I'm not here for your brains but if you've got time I'd also love to share with you the great news of Jesus Christ our Lord and Saviour.

Yep! Check it out:

(Context: Jesus has just died on the cross. Darkness has covered the land for the past three hours. Jesus has cried his final words and given up his spirit to God.)

> At that moment the curtain of the temple was torn in two
> from top to bottom. The earth shook and the rocks split and
> the tombs broke open. The bodies of many holy people who
> had died were raised to life. They came out of the tombs
> and after Jesus' resurrection they went into the holy city and
> appeared to many people. (Matthew 27:51-53)

Now if this isn't one of the craziest things in the stories of Jesus, I don't know what is.

Jesus died on the cross and suddenly the earth shook and all these previously dead holy people came back to life. The passage isn't clear, and neither are the scholars, who it was who came to life. Was it recently dead holy people, the heroes of the faith, or some other group of dead saints? I like the interpretation that it was the old heroes of the faith – Moses, Noah, Elijah, and left-handed Ehud – who all came back to life again. They all yawned, stretched their arms, and came out of their tombs. Then after Jesus rose again, three days later, they went into Jerusalem and made a few celebrity appearances.

The Big Questions

There are a few big questions that need to be asked here. For instance, what the heck were they doing while they were waiting for Jesus to rise again? Did they come to life and then just hang around waiting? Did they wait alone or did they all hang out together? Did they have a dead holy person's convention? (Keynote Address: "Still Relevant – How to Keep

Up to Date with Current Trends When You've Been in the Ground for 3,000 Years"). Did they just get together and play cards and share their favourite Yahweh stories?

And then how did they know it was time to go into the city and visit people? Did an angel come around and say, "Hey guys, zombie embargo is lifted. Have a great time"? Did Jesus come by, shake a few hands and say, "Hey, thanks for coming. It's really great to have you here. Hope you're having fun. Make sure you try the party pies" before they all headed into the city?

And when they entered the city did they just slip in quietly or did they all walk in together in some kind of parade? Did Abraham lead a horde of the previously dead, walking into the city like a protest march of God-botherers still wearing the fashions of the last millennium?

Which makes me think of another question: where did they get their clothes? I suspect whatever they were buried wearing would be just rags at best by then. Did they steal clothes off people's lines? Did they mug a few passers-by? Did they walk around stark naked like terminators just arrived from a spot of time travel? "I used to be dead! You think I care if people see me naked? Where I've been, we don't need clothes!"

And then what did they do when they made it into the city? The Bible says they appeared to people. Did they jump out from behind pot plants or closed doors? "Boo!" "Oh Moses! Stop it! You scared me half to death" "You're telling me, I used to be entirely dead!"

Perhaps they had a PR manager in the city who organised special appearances. "Come see all your favourite Old Testament heroes! Get your Torah signed! One item signed per person – only books and clothing, absolutely no body parts!"

Perhaps they just knocked on doors and asked to come in for dinner. "Hey, remember me? I'm King David. I used to run this town. Mind if I come in for a sneaky falafel?"

And how did anyone know they were holy people? Were they wearing name tags?

And when they finished their public appearances what did they do? Did they go up into heaven with Jesus? Did they go back to their tombs, lie down, and go back to sleep/death? Did they just hang around? Did they all go and get jobs till they eventually died again? I suspect being served at the local kosher deli by Elisha was the first century equivalent of finding Elvis working in a petrol station at some dusty crossroads in the middle of America.

So many questions!

Few Answers

What's amazing is that the Bible answers none of these questions. It talks about this totally crazy thing that happened — one of the most amazing things in the history of the world — and it only gives it two verses! How is that even responsible

Scripture writing? There are a lot of curious people in the world who want answers. Why do we have to wait till we've died and gone to be with Jesus to hear the "Further Adventures of the Previously Dead"?

The fact that Matthew only gives this story two verses within the account of Jesus' death shows how significant the story that it's a part of actually is! If you don't have time to discuss a multitude of resurrected dead people invading a city, then whatever story you are telling must be pretty darn important.

So what is this zombie adventure doing in the Bible? What possible reason could Matthew have for casually referring to a bunch of dead people coming back to life?

The Curtain and the Tombs

In Matthew 27:51 we get a description of the Temple curtain being torn in two. While there is a lot that can be said for the significance of that event, the basic point is that in the past humanity and God were separated because of our sin, but Jesus made a way for us to be in God's presence. The curtain in the Temple separated the people from the holy of holies, the place where God's presence dwelled. The only time people were allowed behind the curtain was once a year, and even then it was only the High Priest, and he always had to bring the blood of an animal with him so that God wouldn't strike him dead (see Hebrews 9:1-10). When Jesus died on the cross, he revealed himself as the true High Priest, offering his life as the one, true sacrifice for sin. God and humanity were no longer separate; Jesus had reconciled them! At the cross Jesus achieved what the priests, Temple, and sacrificial system had not been able to do. The Temple curtain was torn in two, from top to bottom, showing us that now anyone could be in God's presence thanks to the blood of Jesus that makes us holy.

Then comes the craziness of an earthquake and a bunch of holy people rising from the dead. While the Temple curtain being torn showed us something of the power of Jesus' death to unite God and humanity, the rising of hordes of dead people shows us something of the power of Jesus' death to defeat death itself!

Jesus' Retroactive Power

Throughout the history of Israel, all God's holy people, all the Old Testament heroes, and even just the everyday faithful, were trusting, somehow, in the mercy of God to rescue them from death – the consequence of their sin. Over time God had been revealing his character, and there had been some prophecies, but none of these pre-Jesus holy people actually knew the mechanics of how God would save them. All they could do was trust in the character of God.

This is part of what Paul talks about in Romans 4. Abraham (a holy person if ever there was one) did not work to be saved by God, he did not do anything to gain righteousness, he just trusted in God. "Abraham believed God, and it was credited to him as righteousness" (Romans 4:3 quoting Genesis 15:6). What God did Abraham believe in? "The God who gives life to the dead and calls into being things that were not" (Romans 4:17).

Abraham didn't know how God would grant him righteousness, only that he would on the basis of his faith. Every person before Jesus who trusted in God for their righteousness didn't know how God would grant forgiveness and make them righteous; all they could do was trust.

Then along came Jesus: the Son of God, the Lord of the universe, who died on the cross, becoming sin for us so that we might become the righteousness of God (see 2 Corinthians 5:21). Jesus secured unmerited righteousness for all who trust in God's mercy, those who came before him and those who would come after. Jesus is the basis of Abraham's trust, even though Abraham did not know it.

So when all these holy people rose from the dead, it was a sign that the curse of sin had been lifted and Jesus had defeated death. The one in whom all those holy people were trusting had triumphed on their behalf. Now they had been called forth from the earth as witnesses to the saving power of Jesus.

It's as if the sin-crushing, death-defeating power of Jesus' death was so huge that it sent a shockwave throughout the earth, raising people from the dead just by the sheer force of its spiritual magnitude. Jesus' death brings life, and life overflowing, so that people just pop up out of their graves and go out visiting people! That's how powerful Jesus' death and resurrection is.

When we read this excellent story of the boundless power of the cross, it shows us just one more way that the cross is the centre point of all history. Before Jesus sin and death reigned; after Jesus the grave holds no power over those who trust in him. Because of the cross, death is just a temporary pause before we are raised again to life to spend an eternity continuing to live our part in the story of the risen King!

Our Story or "The" Story?

Perhaps there is also something in the fact that, as mentioned before, only two verses are devoted to this amazing dead-raising occurrence. Matthew either has no sense of adventure, or he has razor-sharp focus. He isn't distracted from the literally earth-shattering display of God's love and wrath, saving the world, and shifting the fabric of the universe. If dead people coming back to life only rates a small mention in the story of Jesus' death and resurrection then there is a challenge there for us also. Sometimes we allow things that are much less important than Jesus' death and resurrection to distract us. Sometimes we can think that our story is the central point in the universe, or if not in *the* universe, at very least in *our* universe. But the almost-zombies weren't there for their own sake. They are in the story only because they serve to enhance the wonder of the cross.

I'll tell you what, if I died and then came back to life a couple of hundred years later I'd think I was pretty hot ~~stiff~~ stuff. I'd write a book, I'd call it *Zombie Life: How I Died and Came Back to a Life of Brilliance and Significance.* Then I'd sell the movie rights for a lot of money and make sure that Ryan Gosling played me (a drunk girl once told me I look like him, so I'm owning it). I'd create an undead cookbook (*Five Steps to a Grave-Defeating Diet*) and a fitness program ("Get Abs to Live and Die and Live For"). I'd make sure that rising from the dead was the greatest thing to ever happen to me - I'd milk it for all it was worth! If I found out that my resurrection was just a side effect of some other, more significant guy's death and resurrection, I reckon I'd be pretty unhappy. Not to mention the effect this might have on my book sales.

Here's the thing: if you trust in Jesus, he has raised you to life! Ephesians 2:5 tells us that we were dead in our sin. Dead as a body that's been in the ground for 700 years. We might walk and talk, but spiritually, where it matters, we're dead. But God made us alive with Christ! We have been raised to life. We are no longer dead, we are alive, and alive forever. Death is no longer death, it is just a sleep where our body may decay for a bit. But we'll be alive with Christ, and one day we'll return to get our old bodies back, only they'll be incomprehensibly better – resurrected just like Christ.

And why does all this happen? Is it for our benefit, our wealth, or our victorious life? No. Like the raised people in Matthew serve just to show the greatness of Jesus' death and resurrection, we too exist to show the greatness of our God! We are saved for the praise of God's glory (see Ephesians 1:6)! We were saved so that we might live, not for us, but for God, for the good works that God has prepared in advance for us to do (see Ephesians 2:10). This means that your life, your new life in Jesus, is not about you. You exist only to point to him and serve him. You aren't even going to get a two-verse mention in the Bible. So stop thinking you're hot stuff, and get on with figuring out how in everything you do you might show off the greatness of the God who saved you through his son Jesus. Your life is the result of the overflowing of God's grace that has brought you back from the dead, now you live for him, so make everything you do about him. You work, you rest, you play, you love, you talk, you eat, and you drink all for him! 1 Corinthians 10:31 says, "So whether you eat or drink or whatever you do, do it all for the glory of God." Don't let your life distract or point people away from the life of the God-man who died and rose again for the salvation of humanity and the recreation of the universe. Your story is just a small part of his story.

12

Mark's Nudie Run

Mark 14:48-52

Streaking World Records

Once, at a large sporting match, I found myself wondering what the longest successful streak has ever been at a major sporting event. By streak I don't mean how many times a team has won in a row, but what's the longest a naked person has been able to run around on the field of play without capture. I know it's not an important thing to wonder, I'm not sure if there is anyone who keeps those kinds of statistics. I suspect it's not a world record that many sporting authorities would like to encourage. Perhaps at some point in eternity I'll be able to consult the Heavenly Bureau of Statistics and Records and some efficient angel will be able to look up that fact for me.[1]

---

1 I have a deep hope that this department of heaven exists. There are so many statistics I would love to research. Like how many spiders

So while I suspect I'll never know the answer to that question this side of eternity, what is interesting is that Mark 14:48-52 contains what is perhaps the first ever recorded streaker in history. Mind you, as it is an unintentional streaking, it may be more accurately described as a wardrobe malfunction followed by a naked sprint. However you want to define it, this is an account of a naked man running around during Jesus' arrest, which seems like a really inappropriate time to be naked. When I was a child I used to shower quickly just in case Jesus returned while I was getting clean and I had to stand before the judgement seat of God in the nude. But even being nude on that solemn occasion is nothing compared to being in your birthday suit at the betrayal and arrest of Jesus.

Bible Streaking

The story begins when Jesus, before he was arrested, was eating dinner with his disciples. He was telling them that they will desert him, and he quoted a prophecy from Zechariah saying, "I will strike the shepherd, and the sheep will be scattered" (Mark 14:27). Peter spoke up saying, "Even if all fall

---

did I actually swallow in my sleep? How many Corn Flakes did I eat in my life? How many movies did I watch? How many sneaky farts did I actually get away with, and how many did people smell and know it was me but were too polite to say anything? Apart from my actual death, what was my closest brush with death? And then there are all the statistics from the wider world that would be interesting. How many statistics are actually made up? Were there ever two Scrabble games that were exactly the same? What's the longest wee in history? I feel like I could spend centuries in that department just finding stuff out. I really hope it exists.

away, I will not" (Mark 14:29). I suspect that Peter said what many or all of them were feeling: "The others may be weak, but I'm strong. I'd never desert Jesus."

Jesus knew better. He assured Peter, "Truly I tell you... today—yes, tonight—before the rooster crows twice you yourself will disown me three times" (Mark 14:30). Jesus knew that all of his followers, even the most passionate, were going to leave him. Jesus would go to the cross alone.

Skip forward a few hours and the disciples have lived up to their less-than-stellar reputations. They fell asleep when they should have been praying, one of them betrayed Jesus, handing him over to the Jewish authorities to be crucified, and another got all hot-headed during the arrest and chopped off a guy's ear. Finally, in the face of his arrest, all the disciples, just as Jesus predicted, fled leaving him alone. You can read about all this in Mark 14.

And then comes the corker. Verses 51 and 52 say this:

> A young man, wearing nothing but a linen garment, was following Jesus. When they seized him, he fled naked, leaving his garment behind.

There he is! The streaker to commemorate Jesus' arrest! Sometimes people get naked at concerts or sporting events, but I wouldn't expect a nudie run at the capture of our Lord and Saviour.

The nude runner seems like a weird thing to include in the story. It is perhaps a good indication of the veracity of the gospels that Mark would include this tidbit of information. If you were making up a story about a messiah, why would you include a weird, seemingly irrelevant factoid about a naked guy at the arrest? It's strange little bits and pieces like this that help confirm the Gospels are based on eyewitness accounts.

Who Was the Biblical Streaker?

So who was the guy who ran away naked? Some Bible scholars suggest that this guy was Mark, the writer of the gospel. He wrote himself a little cameo into this Gospel, like the way Alfred Hitchcock put himself in all his films, or Stan Lee appears in every Marvel movie. Perhaps Mark, who was not one of the twelve apostles, had been hanging around with Jesus and his disciples for a while, and then when Jesus got arrested, he was the one who got spooked and ran off in his birthday suit. Maybe Mark was an exhibitionist, and since photos, movies, and social media didn't exist, this was the best way to get his nudity preserved in perpetuity.

Sadly the Bible gives no indication that the naked guy really was Mark, though it'd be cool if it were true. Whoever it was, it would be pretty great to be him, at least afterwards – during, not so much. Like when you have friends who get to be extras in movies, and they'll pause the movie at just the point where you can see their arm on the far right of the screen and they'll say, "That's my arm! That's me! I'm famous!" Perhaps the naked guy carried around copies of Mark's Gospel to show people and then sign it for anyone who wanted an autograph. Perhaps he toured the country preaching and milking his fame as the Exposed Evangelist. That seems like the kind of thing Christians would have loved in the 80s. Don't ask me to justify that last sentence, it's just a hunch I have about late twentieth-century Christians, but they were the ones who had a thing for "Shine, Jesus, Shine". Any group of Christians who regularly sing songs to Jesus commanding him to shine must be a little bit weird. But I digress ...

Whatever the identity of the Starkers Sprinter, what is true is that Mark included it for a reason. He wasn't just writing the gospel thinking, "This is depressing, the hero getting arrested, everyone deserting him. This story needs a bit of moon in moonlight to spice things up!" Mark has something more to say.

The streaker seems to be just one more indication of how alone Jesus was. All his disciples had fled, and even this onlooker was so concerned not to be caught with Jesus that he was willing to leave his expensive clothes behind and flee with all his dangly bits on show. Only one week earlier, Jesus rode into town on a donkey with crowds singing his praises. Now people were willing to sacrifice their dignity to get as far from him as possible.

What's more, the naked guy is probably a fulfilment of Amos 2. In this passage God is speaking about Israel's day of judgement, when they would be punished for their sins. On that day all of the soldiers would run away and "'Even the bravest warriors will flee naked on that day,' declares the LORD" (Amos 2:16).

The fleeing naked man is a sign that the day of God's judgement had come. But instead of the judgement falling on all Israel, it fell on Israel's representative, the one man who could truly represent them and all humanity, Jesus the Messiah.

The truth is, it doesn't really matter who the naked man was, he was left anonymous for a reason. If Mark wanted us to know who it was he would have written it in:

> Nigel the Bumite, wearing nothing but a linen garment, was following Jesus. When they seized him, he fled naked, leaving his garment behind, his hairy, cowardly butt jiggling as he ran away.

The naked guy is anonymous so that we can all identify with him. We too could be the one who ran away; we too are the faithless ones, who will give up even our dignity to escape being caught with Jesus. Jesus was the one man willing and able to go to the cross. Everyone else deserted him.

Abandoning Jesus

When we consider that the streaker could be any of us, we realise there are so many ways we try and escape association with Jesus. Often we do it not by explicitly denying Jesus, just by refusing to own our faith. I find that I can be in a conversation where people are openly mocking Christianity and I'll refuse to speak up and tell them that I'm a Christian. Sometimes it will be people who are talking to me and assume that I agree with them on some point that explicitly goes against what the

Bible teaches and I will just let them believe I agree - I don't want to be seen as one of "those" Christians.

I have watched many people deny their uncomfortable association with Jesus by changing their views on issues so that they are more in keeping with what society expects of them rather than what the Bible teaches. I feel so tempted to do it when it comes to the Bible's teaching on sexual ethics, gender, violence, justice, gossip, revenge, human life, materialism, and so much more. There are some times when society will have a much-needed correction for Christians where we have strayed from biblical standards, calling us back to our main task of love, but most of the time we as Christians stray towards the popular ethics of the time so as not to be confronted with the painful truth that the values of Jesus and the values of the world don't line up.

Sometimes we deny Jesus by acknowledging him with our lips, but living a lifestyle that is totally at odds with what the Bible teaches. We say we want to show that "Christians don't need to be so uptight" when really we don't want the people around us to think that *we're* uptight.

I see this a lot when it comes to drinking. There are many young adults who I spend time with on a Sunday at church, and in Bible studies during the week, and they'll be very committed to Jesus there. But then I hear their stories about the weekend, or I'll see them at a party that we've both been invited to, and it's clear that they see no problem getting drunk. This isn't a one-off mistake, this is a regular decision to drink too much.

The problem is the Bible is pretty clear about drinking (see Proverbs 20:1; Galatians 5:19-21; Ephesians 5:18). As we saw with Noah in Chapter 2 it can lead to some pretty dodgy stuff. But for some reason, there are plenty of followers of Jesus who seem to have no problem disobeying God, and drinking too much, and I suspect part of it is to do with the social pressure they face to drink. It would cost too much socially to be the one person in the group of friends who doesn't get drunk, the one person who is boring and uptight. It's not a denial of Jesus with words, just in choices.

I'm not much of a drinker, but I feel pressure when it comes to entertainment. Sometimes I'll choose not to watch a particular movie or TV show because I don't feel like it'll help me to honour Jesus. When people ask me if I watch it I will say, "Nah. I didn't really like it." Which is probably not true. I probably liked the show, I just don't want to tell people, "I don't watch it because it doesn't help me love Jesus and others." I don't want to seem like a prude and I don't want to be judged for the embarrassing decisions I make because of my faith.

Refusing to acknowledge your uncomfortable associations with Jesus is just an easy way of denying Jesus. The naked man ran away because he didn't want to suffer for being with Jesus. How often do we try to avoid suffering for our association with Jesus? How often do we try to avoid mockery or even having any part of our desired life curtailed by our commitment to him?

It is so comforting to know that even though we might deny Jesus either by the things we say or do, or the things we choose not to say or do, that Jesus does not run away, he does not abandon us. It is only because he refused to deviate from his obedient path, even when it meant suffering and certain death, that we can have forgiveness for deserting him. We can have life because he is faithful when we are faithless.

Jesus the Redeemer

We never meet the Gospel Streaker again, however, we do meet the disciples who fled again. We see them scared in a locked room after Jesus' death. We see them having breakfast with Jesus on a beach after his resurrection. A few weeks after Jesus ascends back into heaven we see them meeting together and praying. We see God fill them with his Holy Spirit. Because of this we see them head out into the streets preaching, leading thousands to faith in Jesus as Lord. We see them healing and performing miracles in Jesus' name. We see them being beaten, and thrown into prison because of their allegiance to Jesus, and we see them still keep telling the world about him. We see them unashamedly go to grisly, painful deaths because they refuse to stop preaching Jesus Christ as the crucified and risen Lord.

Jesus foresaw the disciples' desertion, but he also foresaw their faithfulness by the power of the Holy Spirit. In Mark 13:9-11 he says this to some of his disciples:

> You must be on your guard. You will be handed over to the local councils and flogged in the synagogues. On account of

> me you will stand before governors and kings as witnesses to them. And the gospel must first be preached to all nations. Whenever you are arrested and brought to trial, do not worry beforehand about what to say. Just say whatever is given you at the time, for it is not you speaking, but the Holy Spirit.

Jesus transforms his followers so that they might follow him in good times and bad. That is the power of having God the Holy Spirit living within us. This must give us no end of encouragement. You may see the guy who ran away from Jesus and identify with him. You may be able to list off the many times that you have let Jesus down, the times when you have refused to acknowledge him with your words or your actions. You might feel like a coward when it comes to your faith, but the story of the disciples can show us what our futures can be. You aren't defined by your failures, you are defined by the God who saved you. And the God who saved you lives in you, and he can empower you to stand firm for and with Jesus.

I spent most of my high school life trying not to stand out, and I certainly was very happy if no one knew I was a Christian. I remember once sitting in class and seeing the way my maths teacher was being harassed by the class. The poor guy was friendly but not very popular and kids walked all over him. I thought to myself, "There isn't much I can think of that could be worse than being a high school teacher. The only thing that could be worse is a job where you have to go into schools and tell kids about Jesus. That would be the worst!"

Now my job is to go into schools and tell kids about Jesus. It's nothing spectacular. I'm not one of those Christians in persecuted countries who gets beaten and put in prison, or threatened with death for my trust in Jesus, but I can see in my life that Jesus has changed me and empowered me to do things that used to terrify me.

When we look at Christians around the world, it isn't hard to see plenty of examples of people who are standing up for Jesus. Christians who are willing to lose their jobs, or have their homes taken from them. Christians who are willing to suffer physical harm or go to prison. These are people who have been saved and changed by Jesus, who are willing to suffer because of their allegiance to him. Some of them may be naturally brave people, but I suspect the vast majority are willing to suffer that kind of persecution because it is the Holy Spirit who empowers them.

How to Stand Up for Jesus

You may not be naturally brave, you may not want anyone to know that you're a Christian, but the Holy Spirit can empower you too to be the kind of person who doesn't run away from their allegiance to Jesus. How? Unfortunately there isn't some magic formula, but there are some things that might help you along.

First, pray for boldness. Jesus wants bold people willing to stand up for him, so prayers for boldness are prayers he is willing to answer. Pray before you're in a situation where you might be tempted to disown Jesus or pretend you have no association with him. And then when you find yourself in a situation like that, pray again that God might help you.

Second, remind yourself that you're part of something greater. The disciples stood for Jesus because their ultimate goal was not the preservation of their reputations, their comfort, or even their lives. Their goal was that they might faithfully serve their Lord who faithfully served them so that all people might have the opportunity to be saved. You and I, if we're saved by Jesus, we exist for the same reason. Just knowing you are here for something more than yourself will give you courage to do what's right.

Then finally, do the very thing you want to avoid doing. Speak up, stand firm, be associated with the name of Jesus. As you begin, as you speak, as you stand, as you refuse to run from your Lord, the Holy Spirit will come alongside you, and you'll see that he gives you the words to say, he gives you the power to endure, he gives you the ability to do what you previously thought was impossible so that Christ might be known and glorified. It might be easier to run away, but it hurts a lot more knowing you let down your Lord. It might cost you to follow Jesus, but it's a joy to know you were obedient to your Lord.

I suspect you, like me, can remember many times when you have abandoned Jesus, running like a naked man in the night. But what great news that he has not abandoned us. He went to the cross for us, winning us forgiveness for our unfaithfulness. Now we have his Spirit living in us, and if we let him, he will give us everything we need to stand with him, whatever we might face.

13

The Teleporter
and the Eunuch

Acts 8:26-40

Have you ever seen someone teleport? No? Neither have I, but I'd love to. Better yet, I'd love to be able to teleport myself. That'd be incredible. Generally when people are asked what kind of superpower they want they choose invisibility or flying. I would choose teleportation because it's quicker than flying and less creepy than invisibility.

The Murky Ethics of Teleporting

I once heard an interview with a scientist who said that teleporting is ethically murky. What could be ethically murky about travelling instantaneously from one place to another? He suggested that to achieve teleportation you would need to scan your entire body down to an atomic level then send the information to wherever you wanted to go. At the other end the teleportation machine would have to make an exact recreation of you, right down to the atoms, and there you would appear. However, it wouldn't really be you, it'd just be an exact copy of you, with all the memories of the old you in that old place. This teleported you would be a totally different and new you. The old you would be destroyed, leaving the new you as the only you in the world. Its seems that we can't transport matter instantaneously, but we can transfer information pretty quickly so teleportation would have to function that way. Which makes sense as long as no one was trying to teleport to Australia, in which case it would take ten years for the information to download, assuming it didn't cut out first. Then only half of the person would turn up, the rest of them would be roadkill on the information superhighway.

Seeing as teleportation is essentially suicide and cloning all in one, we need a better solution. Once again, where science falters, God shines, because in the Bible we have the only recorded instance of human teleportation in the history of the world. Now that is something.

Philip Meets the Eunuch

The story begins with an angel telling Philip, "Go south to the road—the desert road—that goes down from Jerusalem to Gaza" (Acts 8:26). Being an obedient guy, off Philip went. While he was on his way he came across an Ethiopian man sitting in his chariot. This guy was an important official of Ethiopian royalty. He was a eunuch, which meant that apart from having his special bits cut off, he was also an important servant, probably a servant of the Ethiopian Queen Mother. In my opinion getting your genitals cut off for a job is a bit extreme. I once moved cities for a job and that was hard enough. You would have to really want the job to mess with your man bits.

This eunuch was travelling from Jerusalem, where he had been worshipping, back to his home. Seeing as he was a eunuch he probably wouldn't have been allowed to worship in the Temple (see Leviticus 21:17, 20), so I'm not entirely sure what he was doing in Jerusalem, just soaking up the atmosphere I guess. In the year 2000 the Olympic Games were held in my home town of Sydney. Unfortunately, I couldn't go to any of the events – not because I was a eunuch, I just couldn't afford the tickets. I did, however, spend a lot of time hanging around the city soaking up the atmosphere. I had a lot of fun enjoying the Olympic vibe. I even enjoyed a concert where a woman weed on the ground next to me. So I imagine this is what the eunuch's experience of Jerusalem was like – enjoying the vibe, avoiding the urine of strangers.

The Holy Spirit told Philip to approach the chariot. When he got close Philip could hear that the Ethiopian was reading from the book of Isaiah:

> He was led like a sheep to the slaughter,
>   and as a lamb before its shearer is silent,

so he did not open his mouth.

In his humiliation he was deprived of justice.

Who can speak of his descendants?

For his life was taken from the earth. (Acts 8:32-33 quoting Isaiah 53:7-8)

Philip asked the guy, "Do you understand what you are reading?" (Acts 8:30). This was a pretty brave thing to do. Imagine you see a rich guy sitting in a limo reading a book. You probably wouldn't feel all that comfortable asking him if he understood what he was reading. He'd probably turn around and say, "Of course I understand what I'm reading. Do you think I'm an idiot? Do you think I just hold books in front of my face to look smart?" And then he'd have his chauffeur beat you up with a copy of said book so as not to show any conspicuous bruises. At least, that's what I do to people who accost me in my limo.[1]

The odds were in Philip's favour that day, however, because the eunuch was feeling humbly ignorant and said to Philip, "How can I . . . unless someone explains it to me?" (v. 31). And then he invited Philip into the chariot.

I suspect this was a big moment for Philip. He was probably hoping to get invited in so he could get a look at the sweet setup the eunuch had going on in there. There was probably a TV, flashing lights on the roof, and a minibar. I would be thinking,

---

1 That's a joke. I don't have a limo or a chauffeur. I have to beat people up all by myself.

"Stay calm. Stay calm. I hope he lets me press some buttons. Stay calm." If Philip was thinking the same thing he managed to keep cool enough to run a Bible study for the Ethiopian right there in the chariot. Philip "began with that very passage of Scripture and told him the good news about Jesus" (v. 35). He would have pointed out to the eunuch how the passage shows a suffering Messiah, and how Jesus came and did exactly what Isaiah prophesied. He would have told him how Jesus was "despised and rejected . . . and familiar with pain" (Isaiah 53:3), how while "we considered him punished by God, stricken by him, and afflicted" (v. 4) he was taking our pain and bearing our suffering. He would have described how Jesus was "pierced" in his hands and his feet "for our transgressions" and "crushed for our iniquities." And he would have made it clear that "the punishment" that was poured out on him "brought us peace" so that "by his wounds we are healed" (v. 5).

Philip would've gone on. He would have shown him how when Jesus went to the cross "he was led like a lamb to the slaughter, and as a sheep before its shearers is silent, so he did not open his mouth" (v. 7). He would have mentioned how Isaiah prophesied Jesus' resurrection when he wrote, "After he has suffered, he will see the light of life and be satisfied" (v. 11). And he would have explained that our sins are forgiven because Jesus "bore the sin of many, and made intercession for the transgressors" (v. 12). Obviously this is why God wanted Philip by the road at that moment, so he would be there just in time to show this man how God had been speaking through Isaiah, 700 years before the arrival of Jesus, of his plans to save the world through the sacrificial death of his son. God works through his timing, and through the obedience of his people, for his glory.

God used Philip's Bible study to convince the eunuch that Jesus is the one Isaiah spoke about, in whom life can be found. The eunuch was so keen that he wanted to be baptised there and then. The eunuch said, "Look, here is water. What can stand in the way of my being baptised?" (Acts 8:36). And he commanded that the chariot stop. They both jumped out (Philip may have stashed away an ashtray as a memento) and into the water they went. Philip then baptised the eunuch. Just as an aside (I promise we'll get to the teleportation very soon), if you think Philip was a Baptist then you believe they were at a deep river and Phil fully dunked the guy, holding him under the water till he almost drowned, releasing him just in time so he could gulp the sweet taste of air, reminding him of the life-giving breath of God won for him by Jesus at the cross. If you think Philip was an Anglican you probably suspect that they just pulled up beside a small puddle that happened to be by the roadside due to recent rain, and Philip stuck his little finger in and dabbed it on the man's forehead, making the sign of the cross so that he would know that he was marked by the cross now until his dying day. I don't want to choose a side here lest some time-travelling religious warrior from the 1500s finds me and executes me for having the wrong views of baptism, but I will say this: if nothing else, it's easier to be an Anglican in a drought.

Tele-freaking-portation

Wherever they are — river, lake, pond, or puddle — one of the craziest things happens next. This is what Acts 8:39 says: "When they came up out of the water, the Spirit of the Lord suddenly took Philip away, and the eunuch did not see him again, but went on his way rejoicing."

What?! Say that again Dr Luke, Author of Acts: "the Spirit of the Lord suddenly took Philip away, and the eunuch did not see him again."

Where did Philip go? "Philip, however, appeared at Azotus and travelled about, preaching the gospel in all the towns until he reached Caesarea" (v. 40).

This is crazy. There they were coming out of the water and suddenly Philip is teleported away. Boom! Puff! Zoom! I don't know what sound it made, maybe a "pop" like he just disapparated, but whatever it sounded like, this is amazing! When Jesus rose from the dead, he kept suddenly materialising all over the place, as if teleportation might be some kind of post-resurrection power. But here Philip has no post-resurrection powers to draw on and he teleports anyway. What a blast! And like many times in the Bible, the most amazing thing happens and the authors tell us almost nothing about it. Why is there not a whole book of the Bible about teleportation? That would be the best! I bet Teleportations 3:16 would be a cracker.

And look at the reactions. Philip disappeared before the eunuch's eyes and the eunuch just "went on his way rejoicing" (v. 39) as if this happened to him all the time. Unless he was friends with Batman I'm pretty sure people didn't just disappear when he was hanging out with them. And what was it like for Philip? Did he know it was going to happen? Did he feel a tingling all over his body till suddenly he was pulled outside of space and time, then wrenched back to 40 or so kilometres from where he was before? Perhaps he had no idea what happened and he was left totally confused; one minute he was in the water, the next minute he was in some entirely different town. What's great is that Philip didn't freak out and spend the next few days contemplating the meaning of life. He just (probably) thought, "Well that was weird" and got on with his job of preaching the gospel!

While the Bible doesn't say much about it, I'm hoping that Philip's teleportation is not an isolated event. Perhaps teleportation is one of the spiritual gifts. Paul does say to "eagerly desire the greater gifts" (1 Corinthians 12:31), and if teleportation is a spiritual gift then it's definitely great and it's definitely worth desiring. If your church is the kind of church where you can receive prayer that God might impart his gifts upon you, go ask for prayer that you might get the gift of teleportation. I can think of many ways that I could move instantaneously from one place to another for the glory of God. I could make a good case for instant transport to pick up a pizza from the local pizza shop being for God's glory. Or, depending on how powerfully I operate in that gift, perhaps I could just appear in Italy to pick up my pizza, giving all the glory to God of course! Catering for youth group events would be so easy and efficient! Intercede for me that I might be a hero of the faith by bending space to my will. I mean, God's will.

Aside from the science fiction (or should we say fact-ion) of this story, there are some other things that are worth noting. I want to point out three things this passage can teach us about personal evangelism (that is, helping the people you know and meet come to know Jesus).

Follow the Holy Spirit

Firstly, follow the promptings of the Spirit. The only way Philip was in the right place at the right time was because he did just that.

One time I was at a party chatting to someone who had found out my job was to teach the Bible for a living. They asked me what my favourite Bible verse was, so I shared that John 16:33 was my favourite, and told them the good news of Jesus and why I trust him even in times of trouble. I went away feeling like a super Christian because I had shared the gospel with a non-believer! I didn't really do anything impressive at all, just answered some questions. It was like they set things up for the perfect evangelism alley-oop. I was in the right place at the right time. I think that's how a lot of our personal evangelism works. People just happen to ask us the right questions and we give ourselves a pat on the back for answering them and being a great and powerful servant of God.

I suspect, however, that God would also like us to be a little bit more proactive. Sometimes that will mean listening to God and doing what he says. The angel told Philip to go to the road, and he did. The Holy Spirit told him to stand near the chariot, and he did. I'm a little uncomfortable reading that. I know if an angel told me to go to a certain road I'd probably do it – what harm can be done by that? But if the Holy Spirit told me to go stand near a chariot, I might refuse. I'd probably feel like some weird creep standing near some stranger's chariot, especially if I could hear what the guy in the chariot was reading.

Sometimes I think I hear the Holy Spirit speak to me and I'll decide if I'm going to obey by how rational or scary it sounds. If it sounds like something I would normally do anyway, you can count me in – "Sure, Holy Spirit, I will go home and have a nap!" However, if it's something that sounds even vaguely confronting like, "Go sit next to that guy with the weird hair," I'll write it off as my imagination and pretend I can serve God just as well sitting next to my friend with normal hair. But if I want to be available to be used by God I have to obey his Spirit. I know I have been blessed by people who have heard the Spirit's prompting and obeyed it. Someone I knew felt prompted by the Spirit to give me $20. At the time I had $4 to my name and $17 worth of travel I needed to do before my next payday. I was very thankful that that person obeyed the Spirit. I wish the Holy Spirit prompted people to give me $20 more often in my life.

I'm sure that sometimes I hear God speaking to me but I think it's just my imagination. Obviously if it goes against what the

Bible says ("Go kick that old lady in the shins") I can be sure that it's not God. But how do I know if I am imagining that I should sit next to the guy with weird hair or not? The Bible has no commands about what sort of people you should sit next to in any situation, regardless of their questionable hairdressing choices. The only way I'll know is if I give it a shot. If I just sit awkwardly next to them for a while, then what have I lost? I've at least been obedient to what I thought might be the Holy Spirit. And if we strike up a great conversation, and I get to show them a bit of God's love, then I've won too! The only way I can lose is if I just ignore it. And the more I obey what I think are God's promptings, the more I'll be able to distinguish what is and isn't God.

If you want a much better chance of being in the right place at the right time, obey the Holy Spirit; we're much better at getting things done when we've got him on our team.

Ask Scary Questions

The second thing we can learn from this passage in Acts is to ask the scary questions. Philip is willing to go up to some random rich guy in a chariot and ask him if he has any idea what he's reading. The guy does not, and wants to know more, so Philip gets to share with him about Isaiah 53 and the whole story of Jesus. The only way this was able to happen is because Philip had the courage to ask what was probably a scary question.

Personal evangelism is full of scary questions. Being willing to ask someone what they think of Jesus, why they aren't a Christian, if they go to church, if they pray, or any other types of questions that might lead to a more substantial topic of conversation than what show you're currently watching on Netflix, is hard. It requires courage, because if you're like me you're afraid that they'll be upset with you for asking something so personal, or they'll mock you for being into Jesus. The truth is that people are less likely to get annoyed at you than you think, especially if you genuinely want to know their answers. If you actually care about the person and want to have a conversation with them rather than try and shove the gospel down their throats, maybe not surprisingly, people are much more likely to want to chat to you.

When I'm walking down the street and I see those people who work for charities, trying to get people to give them money, I usually do my best to look like I haven't seen or heard them. But sometimes they'll try to penetrate my defences anyway. They'll ask me things like, "How are you?", "Do you want to hear a joke?", "Are you concerned about the planet?" or my personal favourite, which I was once asked, "Do you want to save dying children?" How are you meant to respond to that? "No. I want children to die. I'm a monster!" I think I said, "I already do save dying children" and kept walking like a superhero. Anyway, those people ask me questions but they don't care about my response, they just want my money so they can take their commission from the money that I gave for dying children. But if someone I know genuinely cares about me, not just my money, asked me those same questions, I'd have very different responses, and we'd probably have a very interesting conversation.

If you genuinely care about people and you're willing to ask them big questions and have real conversations, you'll have plenty of opportunities to share the hope you have in Jesus. The first step is to ask the relevant questions even if they're scary. See what happens when you ask people what they actually think and feel about the big things in life – you might be surprised what you hear.

Don't Give Up

Finally, don't give up on personal evangelism. We can look at those people who stand up in front of big crowds, preach about Jesus, and then lots of people come down the front and become Christians and we think, "Man, I want to be like that person." At least, that's what I think. However, having had the experience of talking to people who have just responded to a preacher's call, most of them didn't just wander in off the street. Most people who become Christians have, for months or even years, had people praying for them, talking to them, loving them, sharing the stories of Jesus with them, and telling them all about how much God loves them. Their friends and family have done all the legwork, the preacher just gets to take them on the final few steps.[2] Philip didn't say, "Well, I'm not

---

2 Lynne Taylor, a researcher from New Zealand, has looked into this and found that many people who come to faith, who aren't from a Christian background, often do so because of their relationships with people they know who love Jesus. She writes about what she found during her research: "Other Christians played a crucial role in the conversion process. An exposure to Christianity was generally resourced through or, at least enhanced, by engagement with other Christians.

preaching today so I'm not evangelising." He was willing to spend time with one guy by the side of the road and tell him the story of Jesus. You don't need to be a big preacher, you just have to be someone who cares. So, don't give up on personal evangelism; the kingdom of God grows by ones and twos a lot more often than it does by hundreds or thousands.

One Last Thing

One last thing about this story. Christian tradition says that this eunuch was the first Christian in Africa. He took the good news of Jesus back to Ethiopia and through him people all over the country and continent were saved. That is as good a reason as any to keep looking for opportunities to share your faith with the people you come across – you never know what impact your act of obedience will have.

Other Christians invited non-Christians to engage in spiritual practices and they often resourced such engagement. As well as these things that impacted directly on the conversion process, research participants had observed particular things about their Christian friends and colleagues. They saw Christians being helped by their faith; living differently because of their faith; sharing openly and honestly with non-Christians; being deeply hospitable; and allowing room for doubts, questions and complexity in faith. In addition, other Christians helped those I interviewed in various ways. These actions and positive perceptions were significant in the participants' continuing to say 'yes' to the conversion process." Taken from: L. M. Taylor, *Redeeming Authenticity: An Empirical Study on the Conversion to Christianity of Previously Unchurched Australians* (unpublished doctoral thesis, Flinders University, 2017), pp. 230-240. If you want to find out more about Lynne's research you can go to her website – www.lynnetaylor.nz

And if you're still wondering why Philip got to teleport and you and I don't get to, don't stress too much. God will do what he wants. I suspect that bit is in the story to show how powerfully God was using his servants to spread the word of what Jesus had done. If you want one more clue as to how important it is to God that people hear the good news of Jesus, notice that he was willing to bend the rules of science to give Philip more opportunities to tell people the gospel. Sharing this good news of Jesus is pretty important to God – let's make it important to us too.

14

Paul's Killer Preaching

Acts 20:7-12

From Friday 7th to Sunday 9th November 2014 Pastor Zach Zehnder preached the world's longest sermon in Mount Dora, Florida. It lasted 53 hours and 18 minutes. That's probably about 52 hours longer than most pastors would like to preach and 53 hours longer than most churchgoers would like to listen. While Pastor Zehnder was preaching he had a medical team of four nurses who monitored his progress and made sure he was getting enough food and drink while he preached, because marathon preaching is a dangerous business. As it turns out, Acts 20:7-12 makes it clear that marathon preaching can be dangerous to listeners as well. So dangerous, in fact, it's deadly.

The Deadly Sermon

Luke (the writer of Acts) and Paul had arrived in Troas on Paul's third missionary journey. After a week in Troas they went to church and Paul began to teach. Because Luke and Paul were heading off the next day Paul spoke for longer than normal. When I say longer than normal, I mean from sunset to midnight. He would have kept going without a break I suspect, but things didn't quite go according to plan.

There was a guy there sitting in the window named Eutychus. He was somewhere between the age of seven and fourteen. And like any kid that age, he probably found any sermon longer than 15 minutes boring. Deadly boring. "There were many lamps in the upstairs room where we were meeting" (Acts 20:8) so it was probably hot in there with little oxygen. Paul was speaking "on and on" (v. 9) so young Eutychus drifted off to sleep. No one woke him up, they just let him sleep on. I suspect there were some people in the room who envied him. He may have been snoring. He may have been doing that embarrassing thing that you inevitably do when sleeping in public where your mouth is wide open, you're drooling on your chest, and all your friends are taking photos for future birthday posts on social media. Eventually he was so deeply asleep that he slumped over and fell right out the window. This might have been okay, even worthy of a good laugh, had they just been on the ground floor, but they were meeting on the third floor. Poor Eutychus probably had one of those dreams that he was falling only to wake up and realise he actually was falling. Except he didn't realise anything, because he was dead. The writer, Luke, was a doctor so he would have known if he was actually dead, and he assures the readers that Eutychus really "was picked up dead" (v. 9). Death by preaching.

Everyone was probably standing around in shocked horror at what had just happened. One of those moments when a great night goes horribly wrong. The passage tells us that Paul rushed down and threw himself on the boy and said, "Don't be alarmed . . . He's alive!" (v. 10). Verse 11 continues: "Then he went upstairs again and broke bread and ate. After talking until daylight, he left." Which if you look carefully doesn't mean that the boy actually *was* alive. It seems like Paul wanted to distract everyone from what just happened as a result of his preaching, so he threw himself on the boy, told everyone he was alive, shuffled them all back upstairs as if nothing had happened and he hadn't just killed someone, and then said, "Eat! Eat!". It's pretty classic Middle Eastern behaviour to mark every occasion with food, so I guess it's not surprising that that even extends to when you've killed someone with your preaching. Fortunately Luke added verse 12 to make sure we all know that Paul wasn't just pulling a ruse: "The people took the young man home alive and were greatly comforted."

While it is great news that the boy died and God resuscitated him through Paul, it seems risky to me that right after the post-resuscitation snack Paul continued talking for another six or so hours! Had he learnt nothing? Long sermons are dangerous! One person has already died, Paul, let the people get some sleep! But alas, Paul was a man who lived on the edge, he regularly risked life and limb to tell people about

Jesus, even, it seems, when that life and limb weren't his. I am pleased to read that nobody else died for the remainder of the marathon preach.[1] I hope as Paul and Luke headed off for the rest of their journey someone said to Paul, "Thanks for your teaching tonight, you killed it!" And everyone had a good guffaw, even Eutychus who would never fall asleep in a sermon again.

Preachers Relax, Listeners Beware

As a preacher I find this passage very comforting. I have people fall asleep during my preaching all the time. Here is Paul, one of the writers of the New Testament, one of the greatest minds in the history of the world, and people are falling asleep during his talks, so I shouldn't feel too bad when people sleep when I'm speaking. At least I've never killed anyone.

------

1 It would be remiss of me not to mention that the Greek words for Paul's teaching indicate that it may not have been a monologue from Paul for 12 hours, but that there was perhaps more discussion involved, like a Q and A with Paul. Or perhaps as he preached people kept interrupting and asking questions, which meant that a 40-minute sermon took 12 hours. Anyone who has ever led a Bible study with teenagers will understand how this kind of thing can happen. Whatever the case, poor Eutychus was bored stiff. Perhaps he just wished his mum and dad would stop asking questions so he could go home. Maybe he didn't actually fall asleep, maybe he faked the sleep and deliberately fell out the window in an attempt to put an end to the meeting. How disappointing it must have been when he realised that even his own death and return to life was not enough to stop the service and he still had to stay all the way till the end. Poor kid!

However, as someone who can also fall asleep while listening to sermons, I should be very afraid! Falling asleep in a sermon can lead to death – I should be very careful. Listener fatigue is one of the big killers in our churches, right up there with reading the Bible over the speed limit. Perhaps I should go into every sermon with a few emergency Red Bulls on hand in case I start nodding off, fall off my pew, and hit my head, leading to my untimely demise. Still, if I do die in church, I hope the rest of the church does as the people in Troas did: get on with the service and eat some food. Shouldn't let a good church meal go to waste just because I dropped off my perch during a preach.

Sometimes I go to conferences where I listen to Bible teachers for days on end. Many of them are excellent world-class preachers, but I still get sleepy. I think, for safety's sake, Christian conferences should have designated nap breaks lest anyone meet the same fate as Eutychus the Bored.

Perhaps that is the moral to this passage – preachers relax, listeners beware. However, I don't want this to be the shortest chapter in the book so I guess I'll show you some other interesting things going on in this passage.

Early Church Life

The first thing is that it gives us a glimpse into how the early Christians did church together. While Luke doesn't provide a minute-by-minute run sheet, he does make it clear what some of the main elements were. He tells us that they were meeting on a Sunday (the first day of the Jewish week). While the Jewish Sabbath was on a Saturday, the early Christians moved it to match up with the Sunday resurrection of Jesus. For anyone who thinks the resurrection of Jesus was a later invention of Christians, this little piece of evidence says otherwise. When we meet for church on Sunday we're keeping with the millennia-old tradition of God's people, remembering the day Jesus triumphed over death.

Also, it's worth noting how important the teaching of the Word was. The church was devoted to the teaching of the apostles. They were so devoted they listened for hours on end. They were so devoted they kept listening even though, you know—and I don't want to harp on about it—it killed a young boy!

We don't have any apostles like Paul, or Peter, or James, or even B-grade disciples like Thaddeus (whoever he was) to speak to us for hours on end. But what we do have is their teaching in the books of the Bible. We have God's word to us, and we can be devoted to learning about him and about what he did for us in his son Jesus by listening to what the Bible teaches us regularly and faithfully (with plenty of time for power naps if necessary).

The last thing to notice about their time together is that they "broke bread and ate". This almost certainly means that they celebrated communion, and they probably had a meal together too. When we share communion we celebrate and remember Jesus' sacrificial death on our behalf. Jesus commanded his people to continue taking communion together till he returns. The taking of communion focuses and reinforces for Christians what it is that has saved us and makes us children of God. There is no way to be right with God without going through the sacrificial death of Jesus. We do not earn our way into God's presence; we are invited to the communion table to have a meal as family because our brother and Lord has saved us. This is why we keep celebrating communion, because it reminds us of who we are and who has made us so.

Oh, and let's not forget they ate a meal together! If you spend time eating at church, it's biblical. If you want more food at church, tell your pastors that it's biblical. They'll have to listen to you. Start a change.org petition for more chicken nuggets in church – there's no church that can't be improved by a good nugfest (except a vegan church, I guess).

Healing Power

You may be asking, "Why are we talking about how to do church when clearly the most important thing in the passage is that Paul brings a guy back from the dead?" Well, I'm glad you asked. Let's talk about that.

When you look at the incidents of healing in the book of Acts they are almost entirely used by God as an opportunity to bring people to faith in Jesus. One of the apostles will heal someone, sometimes they'll get to preach, and almost always people come to faith in Jesus. However, in the story of Eutychus he is healed and no one becomes a Christian. All the witnesses, as far as we know, were already believers. Instead Luke tells us that the result of Eutychus' dramatic return to life is that "the people ... were greatly comforted" (Acts 20:12).

203

Sometimes God loves to heal Christians, through other Christians, just so that we might know he loves us. What an excellent gift from God to his people that he would comfort us with the miracle of healing. If you get the chance to pray for another believer for healing, you should do it. When you see God at work it is so exciting!

However—and we're straying a little from the story of Eutychus here—we should see healing not just for comfort but as a powerful evangelistic tool. Many times the apostles healed people and then they got the opportunity to explain the gospel. How much more effective would the message of Jesus be if the person had just seen him heal someone? Healing isn't the only way that God affirms the truth of Jesus, but it's a pretty significant tool. If we really want people to know how good Jesus is, why wouldn't we be praying for healing?

Unfortunately for many more conservative Christians (boring ones like me) we don't see healing very often. And the times that we do pray for healing it's almost exclusively for other Christians. We may say that healing is so that people can come to faith in Jesus, but we practise it mostly with people who are already Christians. I know lots of people who have been healed miraculously. All of them were Christians when they were healed. I can't think of anyone who I know personally who was healed when they didn't know Jesus and then came to faith in Jesus. This is probably because praying for people who don't believe in Jesus is scary and they're likely to think you're crazy. I have a suspicion that we should be flipping things around, more like the Acts ratio. We should see healing less as a gift to

Christians so that we might be comforted (though this is good and important) and more as a gift for the world so that many people might believe in the Lord (see Acts 9:40-42).

This is pretty challenging for me. I think I've only ever prayed for healing for non-Christians twice. Once was because a drunk guy asked me to pray for him that he wouldn't have a hangover in the morning (I don't think God answered that prayer, he looked pretty unhappy the next day). The other was for my car, which was healed but never professed faith in Jesus Christ. That's my entire experience of seeing people who aren't Christians healed (or not healed as the case may be).

Now that's not to say that it doesn't happen. I know it does happen. There are countless stories of missionaries healing people in remote communities and many people coming to faith. Or of some of those crazy Christians who feel the Holy Spirit tell them that someone in the supermarket is sick (it's always in the supermarket) and so they go find the person, pray for them, and then right there in aisle three between the baked beans and tinned tomatoes they give their life to Jesus. These are great and encouraging stories. God loves to use healing, not just for comfort, but to bring people to faith in him.

If this sounds right to you, maybe it's time to start praying for the sick, Christian or not. If you're scared of becoming the supermarket guy, then there are some lower-key ways to pray for healing. If a friend tells you they are unwell or injured, tell them you'll pray for them, then check back in with them and see how they're going. If God chooses not to heal them, they'll at least know you are one of God's people and you care. If he chooses to heal them, then you can praise God for the answer to prayer and see what opportunities he presents to share Jesus' love with them. If you're really brave you can ask if you can pray for them right there. After you've prayed check how they're going – if they're healed, great! Tell them Jesus healed them and see what opportunities you get to share Jesus with them. If they aren't healed, pray again, and check again; keep doing this until they're healed, you feel like you should stop, they ask you to stop, or the supermarket closes. If you pray for someone and they don't get healed, don't try and explain it, and don't try and defend God. God has chosen not to heal and that's totally up to him, he's wiser, smarter, and more loving than you. He knows what he's doing.

Of course, all this advice I'm giving you is from very limited experience. So don't listen to me. I'm just telling you what I know from reading books and speaking to people who are braver and more gifted and obedient in this than me. Maybe you should go and find some people who are gifted in healing and love praying for people who don't know Jesus and learn from them. I want to do the same. Perhaps the next book I write will be full of the ways I've seen Jesus heal and save people in grocery stores up and down the east coast of Australia.[2]

---

2 If you want to read a book about this stuff written by people who actually know what they're talking about, try reading *Everyday Supernatural* by Mike Pilavachi and Andy Croft. It's a really easy and practical read helping you understand how the Holy Spirit is at work in the world and how we can join him in what he's doing. There's also no expectation that you have to heal and convert an entire supermarket,

So if I can sum up what we've learnt from this passage, it's this: God heals so that his people might be comforted and so that the world might come to a saving knowledge of Jesus. Healing is a physical gift that leads to an even greater spiritual gift. God's people should be willing to pray for healing for people who know Jesus and people who don't. And God's people should meet together to devote themselves to the teaching of the apostles, celebrate communion, and share food (preferably nuggets). Finally, preachers shouldn't preach too long, and listeners shouldn't listen to sermons while sitting in windows. Let Eutychus be an example to you – listening to a sermon can be a dangerous activity.

which is comforting. (M. Pilavachi and A. Croft, *Everyday Supernatural*, Colorado Springs: David C Cook, 2016.)

15

Paul's Cutting Comments

Galatians 5:12

Great Rivalries of History

If I asked you to think of the great rivalries of history, what would you think of? Perhaps Batman and the Joker, or Superman and Lex Luthor, The Avengers and the other Avengers, Harry Potter and Voldemort, the Jedi and the Sith, Sherlock and Moriarty. Maybe you'd be thinking outside the realm of popular culture and into the real world – Apple and Android, Xbox and PlayStation, Coke and Pepsi, choccy milk and strawberry milk, people who use Comic Sans and people who have taste, people who know how to use quotation marks and "people" who don't.

In this last passage we're dropping into one of the great rivalries of history. The Apostle Paul *vs* people who think frozen yoghurt is just as good as ice cream. Actually, that's not true. It's Paul *vs* the Judaizers, who may or may not have had an opinion about frozen yoghurt.

These Judaizers (whom he refers to as agitators) made Paul so angry that he said he wished they'd cut their genitals off. Paul literally said that. Look, right there in Galatians 5:12:

> As for those agitators, I wish they would go the whole way and emasculate themselves!

Wowzers! Paul *was* angry. If you want to fully appreciate this fight, read on and I'll tell you all about it. It's going to need a little bit of background but there'll be drinking, parties, and sweaty Albanians, so you should be okay.

Pagan Fun Times

There are some ungodly religious practices in the Bible that seem pretty fun. For instance, a lot of the people groups surrounding Israel would have had religious festivals that consisted of getting drunk and having sex with prostitutes. Now, I don't endorse that kind of behaviour, but were I not a follower of Jesus, a religion of sex, alcohol, and parties would sound pretty appealing. It'd be like living the life of a newly minted first year university student all the time, secure in the knowledge that there was a god who was looking fondly on all your bonking and barfing.

I guess plenty of people would say, "Why do you need a god to endorse those things? If you like it, do it!" That works for some people, but when you look at humanity across the ages, we all have this great need to connect with the divine, to ascertain what will appease and please the gods and goddesses. The expression of this need manifests itself in different ways. Sex, feasts, drinking, starring in *Mission Impossible* films, these seem like religions tailor-made by humans to make themselves happy.

> Religious Person 1: What do you feel like doing at temple today?
>
> Religious Person 2: If I could do anything it'd be eat a bunch of food, drink a lot of alcohol, and then have sex with some of those temple workers.
>
> Religious Person 1: I was thinking we might say a few prayers and burn a bit of incense, but your idea sounds like more fun. Let's do that!

As fun as that all seems, the sex and party religions are generally much less popular than religions that make life difficult for us. If you look at religions around the world people tend to do all sorts of difficult things because they think it will impress their god. For some reason we're just sure that the gods want us to be unhappy. We seem to keep thinking that they really enjoy seeing us self-flagellate, deny ourselves sex, refuse to eat food, go on long pilgrimages, feel guilty, and in extreme cases sacrifice our children.

This way of doing religion is a lot less appealing, but for some reason humans often do religion like that. I'd pick the sex and drink religion any day.

Unfortunately one doesn't really get to pick their faith based on which religion has the best stuff on offer. Picking a religion is not like picking holiday accommodation where the choice is between a five-star hotel in the Bahamas or an Airbnb where two sweaty Albanians have rented out the space between them in their king single. That choice is obvious, you pick the one that is more fun. But you can't do that with religion; one might look more fun, but it may also just be a human invention and following it earns you the wrath of God/gods. So it's more like when you book your holiday, you have to choose the hotel or the Albanians, except if you choose the wrong one you get eternal damnation. If that's the case you're going to get online and check out the reviews: "I thought I would be sipping cocktails in one of those fancy bars that are in the pool, but when I arrived at my hotel I found out I was actually in hell. 0 stars."

I'm not booking a trip to the Bahamas if the Bahamas is actually a lake of eternal fire, no matter how good the brochure looks!

Okay, this may seem like a bit of a tangent – all I'm saying is you don't get to pick your religion based on what's fun, you pick it based on what's true.

"Ahh," you say. "I'm ready for this. I know what's true, it's Jesus!"

I tend to agree with you. Seeing as Jesus claimed to be God, did a bunch of miracles, died and rose again, that would probably be a good indicator that Jesus might have been onto something.

In the great religion rivalries what did Jesus advocate? Which team was Jesus on? Sex and parties, or flagellation and unhappiness?

Neither. Jesus is all about trust and relationship.

Jesus taught that he is the way, the truth, and the life (see John 14:6). He taught that we need to come to him to receive life (see John 4:13-14). He taught that he has the power to forgive sins (see Mark 2:1-12). His disciples, whom he tasked with spreading his message, taught that if you want to be saved, you trust in him (see Acts 4:8-12). You don't need to do crazy stuff to make the gods happy. You place your trust in the mercy of God, shown at the cross.

What saves a person? Jesus. Not drinking, partying, or sexing. Not fasting, punishing, or sacrificing. Only Jesus. Jesus has done all the unpleasant things necessary, and they aren't just weird human-made ideas to make some human-made god happy. He did everything needed so that we might live a life that honours God, to live the way humans were created to live, not just satisfying our base desires. He lived a life of total love, and then he died a death worthy of one who had done everything wrong. As a result we who have done it all wrong can be treated by God as if we have done everything right. All we need to do is trust Jesus.

Salvation is simple, it's found in Jesus and only Jesus.

But no matter how simple things are, we just love to make things a little harder for ourselves. We just can't be convinced that God doesn't want us to make life unnecessarily difficult.

The Judaizers!

Now it's time to meet Paul's old rivals. Enter the Judaizers!

While the Judaizers sound like they could be some Hasidic hip hop group, they aren't. They were a group of Jews who were hanging around just after Jesus died, rose again, and went into heaven, and were a part of the newly formed Christian church. They knew about Jesus, they believed that he died on the cross for our sins, but they weren't that keen on Jesus abolishing the requirements of the Old Testament law, and they especially didn't want their old-time rivals, the Gentiles, being just let into this new Jesus-worshipping sect of Judaism without having to adhere to its basic rules.

They wanted people who started following Jesus to also be compelled to be circumcised, to not eat pork, not wear clothes made of two different fibres (see-ya, yoga pants!). They were saying, "Yeah, look, Jesus is awesome, he died for our sins, but we can't just throw out all these laws God gave us – they're perfectly good laws, especially circumcision. People should trust Jesus, and be circumcised!" Why? Because the old laws were very good at letting you know who was on your team and who wasn't. Your identity was wrapped up in these laws; to get rid of them would be to get rid of part of who you are. So they tried to insist that every new male believer should be circumcised.

Uncle Paul Gets Angry

Some people might have wondered what the big deal was, but not Paul. Paul knew that this was a big problem, because if you say salvation is reached through Jesus *plus* obeying the Old Testament law, you're not trusting in Jesus and only Jesus.

Paul said that if you want to be circumcised you are obligated to keep the whole law! Every single law in the Old Testament you had to keep, and keep it perfectly. If you couldn't do that you'd be condemned by the law. If you start relying on circumcision to save you, you stop relying on Jesus to save you. This is what Paul says in Galatians 5:2-3:

> Mark my words! I, Paul, tell you that if you let yourselves be circumcised, Christ will be of no value to you at all. Again I declare to every man who lets himself be circumcised that he is obligated to obey the whole law.

Paul is getting really angry about this. He's angry because these people are trying to minimise the sacrifice of Jesus. He's angry because they want to play a part in their own salvation. He's angry because, while for them it might be about identity, for him it's about people's eternities; they're leading people astray and shutting people out of God's kingdom. These are all valid reasons to get angry.

On top of all this, these people who are preaching the circumcision are pretending that Paul is on their side. They're saying, "Just ask Paul, he agrees with us!" He had no desire to be used to endorse the message of the people who are preaching the opposite of him. So finally he loses it and says this in Galatians 5:11-12:

> Brothers and sisters, if I am still preaching circumcision, why am I still being persecuted? In that case the offence of the cross has been abolished. As for those agitators, I wish they would go the whole way and emasculate themselves!

Yeah! Take that!

Paul is saying, "As for you stirrers, if you love circumcision so much, why don't you just go ahead and cut everything off, the whole sausage and potatoes! I wish your knives would slip and you'd junk your junk!"

This is impressive! Paul is not holding back.

Now I'm guessing you've never heard your pastor express any desire for anyone to cut off their genitals. I suspect if they did, there would be more than a few angry emails, and probably an emergency church meeting or two. You could probably even be fired for saying something like that.

So why can Paul get away with it?

Well, for a start, the early church leaders were a pretty loose bunch of fellas. Peter, the great apostle, once cut some dude's ear off, Mark went for a nudie run,[1] and Paul used to murder Christians. These church leaders weren't exactly the most reputable bunch. So when Paul says something like this I suspect all the Galatians just said, "Classic Paul, always bringing the zingers!" rather than writing a furiously worded papyrus.

God Cares About the Problem

And here's the thing, the fact that God allowed this bit of uncouthery into the Bible must mean that he's happy for it to be in his Word. We all expect God to be respectable, but he's not so concerned with fitting in with our expectations that he speaks like your Methodist grandmother. God is interested in truth, he's interested in life, and if there is anything that we've learnt in the previous fourteen chapters of this book, it's that God isn't afraid for things to get a bit crazy. God isn't going to let a little thing like civilised discussion get in the way of telling people who he is and how you can have life in him.

Let's be totally clear. Paul is getting angry because what he is discussing is at the heart of the gospel. Either Jesus saves

---

1 Perhaps. See Chapter 12.

you, or your good works save you. There is no middle ground. Remember the Albanian Airbnb? This truth is the difference between salvation and God's judgement, so it's appropriate that Paul says some inappropriate things! What's more inappropriate, Paul's talk about people getting their penises cut off or people preaching lies so that their followers miss out on the grace of God and end up going to hell? This is worth getting angry about. In the first chapter of Galatians Paul is so clear that this is a big issue he tells his readers that if even an angel preaches a false gospel they should be eternally condemned (see Galatians 1:8-9).

We Should Get Angry Too

We might feel uncomfortable with this but sometimes we should get angry too! I am one of the calmest people I know. I rarely get angry about anything. This is a pretty good skill to have when stuck in traffic, or when dealing with customer service employees after being on hold for an hour, or when leading a Bible study full of twelve- and thirteen-year-old boys. But other times it's not that helpful. For instance, when something that should actually make me angry happens (like someone distorts the gospel) I say things like, "Oh dear. That's not good. That's quite annoying." Perhaps I should be willing to take a page out of Paul's book and demand a few castrations or something.

There are some things worth fighting for and one of those things is the gospel. If we get this wrong or other people distort it, God's glory gets tarnished and people's eternities are put in jeopardy. The good news is that God has done everything possible and everything necessary to make a way for us to be right with him and saved to eternal life. This is worth fighting for and it's worth getting angry about. It's worth protecting this truth from distortion and corruption. Now that doesn't mean that if someone preaches a false gospel we get a licence to do whatever we want. We shouldn't burn down their house, slander them on social media, or even castrate them! But we should oppose the false gospel, with truth and love. We should pull people aside when they're teaching things that aren't in line with the gospel we read in the Bible and show them where we think they've strayed from the truth. We should speak up publicly when they aren't interested in listening to us privately. The truth is, truth is worth getting angry about.

Gospel Love

What's more, if this gospel is worth getting angry over then it's worth getting excited about. If you're like me, and not much makes you angry, you may also be like me in that not much makes you excited. Some things do of course excite me; important things like baked potatoes, roast potatoes, mashed potatoes, or cute babies named Potato. However, the fact that God has saved me from hell by sending his son to die in my place, so that now I can trust in him for salvation rather than in my own goodness, is even more fantastic than even the greatest of all potato dishes. It's worth singing about and telling your friends about. It's worth shaping your life around and devoting your life to. The gospel is the greatest news of all time, it's worth anything and everything you give for it.

Some people are really good at getting angry about the gospel, but they don't love it at all. Those people love being right more than they love the gospel. Some people are really good at getting excited about the gospel, but they aren't willing to confront people who preach and teach it wrong. These people like being loved more than they love the gospel. When we truly love the gospel we will be enthralled enough by it to celebrate it at any available opportunity, and we'll be protective enough of it that we'll defend it whenever necessary, despite what it may cost us.

If this sounds good to you, then the solution isn't really to nurture your feelings of anger when someone says something wrong. For instance, you shouldn't turn on your TV at 5 a.m. on a Sunday and wait for those preachers who want you to give them money for their next private jet, then hurl insults at your TV. That won't help you, them, or your sleeping neighbours. Nor should you just try and be more excited about Jesus by, say, running down the front during every worship song at church and jumping around in the hope you catch those excited feelings.

No, the solution is to know the gospel more. Spend your time reading your Bible, and contemplating what it means for Jesus to save you. Read the Gospels and marvel at who Jesus is and what he did for you at the cross. Read Romans and consider how sinful you are, and how great God's love is. Read Ephesians and be moved by the power of Jesus and the wonder of grace. Read Revelation and be confused by the dragon and plagues, but then be comforted that the end of the story is that Jesus wins, and he's bringing us home. Don't just read about it in the Bible, ask other followers of Jesus how he has changed their lives through his love and mercy. Pray that God might help you know that this good news is not good news in general but good news in particular – it's good news for you. As you know the good news that Jesus' death and resurrection is for you, you'll fall more in love with the gospel, and be moved to be excited by it and defensive of it, whatever the need may be. Anything else just won't cut it (see what I did there?).

The End Bit

This is the end. Well done on making it all the way here. Or well done on skipping to the back of the book.

I'm not entirely sure this book needs a conclusion. It's not like I have written some great thesis that needs summing up.

I guess my hope is that in reading this book you've seen how good the Bible is. It's full of some crazy stuff, and people doing some pretty weird things. Even God acts in ways that seem strange, but in it all we see him weaving it all together to tell the big story of his love for the world.

The other thing I hope you've seen is how important Jesus is to everything. I kept coming back to Jesus in this book because as you read the Bible you discover that everything comes back to him. Many of the stories we looked at showed us how easily humans get it wrong. And yet, despite the Bible's (and the world's) ample evidence of the stupidity, selfishness, and evil of humanity, we still have a God who would send his son Jesus to die for us to give us life. The very centre of Christianity is that God would become a man to save humanity, dying in our place, for our sins, and rising again to new life so that we too might one day rise like him. We don't deserve this kind of love, but we get it anyway. That's how good God is.

I hope this book has also challenged you to live in response to this love. We do not need to earn God's love, but we do get to live out God's love. Jesus didn't just come to save the world but to change the world. You and I, we get to join Jesus in bringing his kingdom to earth, in loving others, our neighbours, the poor, our enemies, and our friends.

If you're the kind of person who didn't read the Bible much before reading this book, I hope you'll keep reading the Bible now. I hope you'll go on to read all those stories and passages that may not make you laugh, but that will show you more of the God who loves you.

If you're the kind of person who read the Bible a lot before reading this book, then good on ya mate! Keep it up! You probably know as well as or better than me how much gold there is in there.

As I leave you I'm mindful that chances are you have your own stories to tell of nudity, poo, farts, and other bodily functions. I hope a few of you even have stories of talking animals and teleporting too. Some of these stories are funny and you tell them to your friends. Some of them may fill you with shame and you don't mention them to anyone. Let me encourage you that, just as the weird, crude, funny, and nude passages from the Bible have shown us more of God's love for us in Jesus, as you reflect on your life you'll see the same thing. God has been showing you his love in some very unexpected ways, if only you would look. I hope that you can love your stories as much as I love these stories because they show you Jesus. And I hope that you might be willing to share with others what God has done in you, and what God has done in the world through his son, so that everyone might know that we have a God who loves us at our weirdest, crudest, funniest, and nudest.

What's Next?

1. Connect with Tom

If you enjoyed *Weird, Crude, Funny, and Nude* and want to stay up to date with Tom, learn when new books are coming out, get blog updates, and more, sign up to his mailing list at tomfrench.com.au.

While you're there you can also subscribe to his podcast, watch his videos, access his sermons, and more!

If you want to connect with Tom directly to let him know what you think of the book, or just to say hello, email hello@tomfrench.com.au.

2. Review the Book

The best way you can help this book be seen by others is by giving it a review. Write an honest review of the book on Goodreads, Amazon, on your blog, Instagram, Facebook, in your local school newspaper, on a telegraph pole, or anywhere else you'd like.

3. Get Tom to Speak

Tom is a sought-after communicator for young people. If you would like to book him to speak at your youth group, church, camp, school chapel, conference or Senate inquiry visit tomfrench.com.au/booking.

4. Get Tom's Other Book

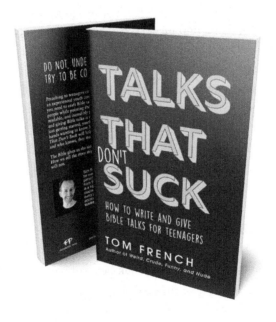

Available now at tomfrench.com.au

Acknowledgments

Sometimes I start reading acknowledgments for a little while and then realise they're just a bunch of people the author is thanking. If this is at the beginning of the book, I skip straight to the actual content. If it's at the end of the book I stop reading immediately and pat myself on the back for finishing a book.

So first of all I'd like to thank you for reading this bit of the book. If you stay till the end I'll thank you again.

Before I go any further I need to acknowledge everyone I told I was writing a book who didn't laugh at me. Writing has felt like a foolish endeavour – who would be willing to read 50,000 words written by me? It was always encouraging when people heard about the book and said, "That sounds great!" even if they were just pretending.

I'm quite indebted to Graham Stanton and the late Andy Stirrup who taught me at Anglican Youthworks College to read, understand, and teach the Bible to young people. Hopefully people reading this book don't feel it reflects the level of maturity of the college's graduates. There are many more learned and mature graduates achieving big things for the gospel in the world.

In 2003, on my first day of work as a new youth minister in a new church, I was sent to Soul Survivor's annual conference in Sydney. My new boss was running the thing. He put me in charge of running sumo wrestling with people wearing the inner tubes of old car tyres. It was a great first week of work; till that point I hadn't encountered anything like Soul Survivor. I'm very thankful for what has become a life-changing association. Over the years I have been given more and more responsibility. It was at Soul Survivor that this book first began in the form of a seminar called "The Bible Makes Me Giggle". I am glad that I was allowed, and even encouraged, to explore these strange and hilarious passages of the Bible, and invited back year after year. The Soul community (in Australia and abroad) has been a source of constant encouragement. Listening to Mike Pilavachi preach in those early years taught me a lot about how to preach, and now write – plenty of fun but plenty of truth. I am very thankful for Matt Gelding, who has been a friend and mentor, and who has believed in me and this book from day one.

Over the years I've been blessed to get to lead youth ministries in a number of different churches. Getting the chance to hang out with teenagers, play dumb games, have good conversations, teach the Bible, and see them meet and grow in their love for Jesus is an exceptional privilege. For every young person who has come through a ministry I have led, either for a few hours, or for years, you guys taught me so much about life, and Jesus, and the world. Much of what I have learned from you has shaped this book.

For most of the time I was writing this book I was working for Crusaders. I'm so blessed to have had the chance to teach the Bible to thousands of young people every year and hone my gifts. I'm still stoked that CRU would let me represent them. Schools Ministry team, past and present, you're the best. Peter Crawford, it's been a blessing to have worked for you, thank you for trusting me and being one of the best bosses I've ever had (twice!). Clare Wimble, everyone needs a Leslie Knope, I'm glad you've been around for so long to cheer me on, and keep encouraging me in Jesus. Sorry I left, twice.

The readers who read drafts of this book gave me such helpful insight. Chris Morphew, thanks for the New Year's Eve insights, they gave me plenty of confidence – after all, you know what you're talking about. I hope we get that podcast recorded. John Buckley, thanks for making sure I haven't written heresy. If I get arrested by the church police, I'm taking you with me. Andreana Reale, I'm so glad you gave me your Jesus-loving, feminist, progressive insights, I needed your wisdom and push back. Dan Odell, what a man! You had so many important thoughts and suggestions. If you happen to read this book again, I hope you see the improvements you made. And to all those of you who said you'd read the book but never got back to me, I understand, I still haven't replied to Katy's email where she asked for feedback on her script. Sorry, Katy. Anyway, thanks for your willingness.

Sam Williams, a youth who has transitioned to friend, thank you for using your graphic design talents to typeset this book. I appreciate the generosity of your time and skills. As I write this I actually have no idea what the book will look like, but faith is evidence of things not seen, and I definitely have faith that as people read this, it's looking spiffy!

Angus Olsen, my Youthworks friend, your illustrations are amazing! I'm so pleased you brought your skills to this and were willing to draw so much vomit for the sake of the gospel. Thank you for putting up with all the changes and my lack of experience in knowing how this is done. One day I definitely will visit you and buy a coffee from you. (Actually, I don't drink coffee.)

I never really knew what a book editor did until I had a book editor edit my book. Jo Stockdale, you're the best editor I've ever had. I'm very grateful for your insight, questions, suggestions, and changes that have made this book so much better. I'm glad you know what you're doing. Thanks for being so speedy too, and working to my ambitious deadlines. I'm so glad you got what I was doing.

Hsu-Ann Lee, thanks for your thorough proofreading. I hope my typos didn't stress you out too much. Typos are my spiritual gift.

There was a pretty significant family crisis towards the final stages of getting this book done. Thank you everyone who looked after us, brought us meals, washed clothes, visited, sent cards, flowers, and all the rest. I'm sure this book would have disappeared for a long time if we didn't have such good friends and family (genetic and Christian) to look after us.

I'm really blessed to have such a great family - Mum, Dad, Hannah, Jo, Victor, Sebastian, Hugo, Steve, and Valentina. You've challenged me, cared for me, and are probably the main people buying this book. Thank you for being my best supporters and loving me.

Emily, Wife, you're the best. I like you and I love you. I couldn't have done this without your constant encouragement, excellent jokes, wisdom, and insight. I'm glad you read this book before anyone else did and still liked me afterwards.

God — Father, Son, Holy Spirit — there is no way to adequately acknowledge you and all you've done. Thanks for saving me and loving me, and giving us the Bible that I get to read, explore, and teach every day. All glory to you.

Lastly, to those of you readers who are still reading, good on ya! You da real MVP.

About

Tom French is married to his excellent wife, Emily Sandrussi. He is also a youth ministry veteran, having spent over sixteen years working with teenagers in churches and schools around Australia. Every year he teaches the Bible to thousands of young people in youth groups, churches, schools, and camps throughout New South Wales and Victoria. He has a Bachelor of Theology from Sydney Missionary and Bible College. Tom lives in Melbourne with Emily. You can often find him at the movies eating popcorn for dinner.

Visit tomfrench.com.au to sign up for regular blog updates and the latest on new books. There you can also listen to Tom's sermons, book Tom to speak, see a photo of Tom holding a microphone, and much more.

Follow Tom on Facebook: facebook.com/twfrench
Follow Tom on Instagram: @twfrench
Subscribe to Tom's Preaching Podcast: Search for "Tom French" in your favourite podcast app

About the Illustrator

Angus Olsen is a Disney trained cartoonist and illustrator. Angus studied theology at Youthworks College and spends most of his time making coffee from his tiny cafe kiosk in Katoomba in the Blue Mountains, NSW.

Follow Angus on Instagram: @cafexpresso_comics

Made in the USA
Monee, IL
19 December 2019